SKY ROADS OF THE WORLD

Amy Johnson's story about her adventurous flying career

by

Amy Johnson

Trotamundas Press Ltd.
The Meridian, 4 Copthall House, Station Square, Coventry
CV1 2FL, UK

"Sky roads of the world" by Amy Johnson

First published in 1939 by W.&R.Chambers, Ltd.

ISBN: 978-1-906393-18-2

Trotamundas Press is an international publisher specializing in travel literature written by women travellers from different countries and cultures.

Our mission is to bring back into print great travel books written by women around the world which have been forgotten. We publish in several languages.

It is our privilege to rescue those travel stories which were widely acclaimed in the past and that are still relevant nowadays to help us understand better the diversity of the countries and the world.

The travel stories also make an enjoyable reading, full of adventure and the excitement of discovery.

We are proud to help preserving the memory of all those amazing women travellers which were unjustly forgotten and hope that you will enjoy reading about their interesting experiences as much as we have enjoyed researching them.

www.trotamundaspress.com

Amy Johnson
(1903-1941)

Amy Johnson was born on 1st July 1903, the eldest of John and Amy Johnson's four daughters. She grew up in Hull, Great Britain, where her father ran a prosperous fishing business. In 1922, Amy went to Sheffield University where she graduated 3 years later with a bachelor's degree in economics. Afterwards she returned to Hull and worked briefly at two local offices. But in 1927 she decided to move to London to find better opportunities. Amy moved into a YWCA hostel and began to look for work. She took a brief job as a shop assistant before starting work as a secretary for a law firm.

A year later Amy decided to take up flying but was initially put off because of the expense. However, one day she decided to take a bus ride to Stag Lane aerodrome and there she learned that she could join the club and learn to fly at a fraction of the cost given to her by the local flying school. She had to wait through a five month waiting list and eventually took her first lesson on 15 September 1928.

Amy Johnson made her first solo flight on 9 June 1929. But as things began to look up at the aerodrome, her supervisor at the law firm gave her an ultimatum that she must either quit her job or quit flying. A month later, Amy's father agreed to her request for financial support and Amy quit the law offices. During her time at the aerodrome, Amy had also been learning about aircraft mechanics and eventually became the first woman in Britain to earn a ground engineer's license.

The idea to fly solo to Australia came to Amy as she was eager to earn publicity both for aviation and for herself, hoping that it would lead to job offers. Bert Hinkler's 1928 record flight from England to Australia still stood and no woman had yet attempted to challenge it. Amy decided to take the plunge and started looking for a sponsor but her many appeals to wealthy potential backers proved fruitless until March 1930, when her plea for assistance to Sir Sefton Brancker, the Director of Civil Aviation had a positive response. He wrote to aviation benefactor Lord Wakefield of Wakefield Oil on her behalf and on April 1930 Lord Wakefield met with Amy Johnson and agreed to provide the necessary backing for her

challenging flight. Amy's father had already agreed to provide 500 pounds.
A suitable plane was eventually found. It was a two year old de Havilland Moth already fitted with extra fuel tanks and she christened it Jason, after the registered trademark of her father's fish business and had it painted green with silver lettering.

On 24 May 1930, after flying 8,600 miles from London in nineteen and a half days, Amy arrived in Australia to great fanfare there and in Britain. Her return to England on 4 August brought even more publicity. The Australia trip was Amy's finest hour, although she later made record breaking flights, namely to Japan in 1931, to Cape Town in 1932 and again in 1936 to Cape Town. But long distance stunt flying was becoming familiar and the most noteworthy obstacles had been conquered by then.

Amy Johnson and the fellow aviator Jim Mollison married in July 1933. Jim was a playboy, a womaniser and a heavy drinker. They tried to keep their careers and marriage going with joint flights and solo endeavours, but Jim's infidelities, absences and too much press drove the couple apart. They divorced in 1938 and Amy resumed her maiden name.

Amy's passion for flying cooled after learning that her friend Amelia Earhart had disappeared while flying over the Pacific Ocean in 1937. Money was tight and she tried to live a quiet lifestyle in the country. Amy took up gliding and became an ardent supporter of the sport.

When World War II erupted, Amy wanted to contribute to the war effort and in 1940 she joined the Air Transport Auxiliary delivering military aircraft from factories to air bases. On Sunday 5 January 1941, Amy took off from the Blackpool aerodrome in a twin-engine Airspeed Oxford and headed for Kidlinton Airbase in Oxfordshire. According to newspaper accounts, she was not seen again until 4 hours later when she parachuted out of her plane over the icy waters of the Thames estuary. She ditched her plane near a convoy of British ships. Sailors threw lines to her but she couldn't grasp them. The ship HMS Haslemere's commanding officer Lieutenant Commander Walter Fletcher tried to help her but succumbed to the cold and lost consciousness before his body was picked up. Amy's body was never found.

The mystery of her death led to many stories in the press about the causes of her disappearance. But whatever the circumstance of her death, nothing can disminish what Amy Johnson accomplished as a pioneer aviator through her iron will and sheer determination to succeed. Her legend was thus born.

DEDICATION

This book is dedicated to all those who fell by the airwayside, for nothing is wasted, and every apparent failure is but a challenge to others

CONTENTS

Chapter I

THE DAWN OF THE AIR AGE

It is generally admitted as an axiom that civilisation develops in proportion as transport facilities improve. Countries which to-day still use donkey transport occupy the same status in the world that we ourselves occupied over a thousand years ago. Fast transport means facilities for trading, for travelling and getting to know our neighbours, for the interchange of ideas and customs, for the exchange of goods, raw materials, and foodstuffs. In this hurrying modern world it is very evident that the slow-thinking, slow-acting countries will be left behind in the race for power and precedence.

We are living to-day in the Air Age, and ours is one of the leading nations in our present civilisation because we have realised—slowly, but none the less surely—that to neglect this new, swift, vital means of transport would be the first quick step to our downfall.

For centuries man has felt an urge to fly, without quite knowing why. Certain it is that he cannot have visualised flying as a means of commercial transport, carrying loads of passengers and goods at incredible speeds over all the wide earth. It is far more likely that he merely envied the birds their freedom and wanted to be able, like them, to shake off the fetters of gravity and soar far afield, adventuring into space.

The earliest attempts to fly were all based on efforts to copy the movements of birds. Flapping wings, and even feathers, played their part in the very earliest contraptions, but never was man able to fly like a bird, and his struggles led only to failure and death.

Balloons, of course, flew more than a century ago, but the principle was simple, and the mere act of rising into the air with a hot-air balloon was no extraordinary achievement. The harder part, indeed, was to come down again! Nor could balloons, however successful at going up and coming down, ever be of any commercial use, drifted hither and thither as they were at the mercy of the elements.

What was wanted was a machine that would take off by its own power within a reasonable distance, fly straight to a predetermined destination, and glide down to land safely, also in a reasonable distance.

At the end of the nineteenth and the beginning

of the twentieth century, many active brains were puzzling over the problems of flight. A German, Otto Lilienthal, made a glider which flew through the air and glided down to land, but, without an engine, it was powerless to take itself off or to stay up. He then built an engine and fitted it into his glider, but he had tried the Fates too far, and they mercilessly sent him crashing to his death on his first trial flight.

About the same time were a few enthusiastic Englishmen working on similar lines, and two or three Americans. Each had his own ideas, and it was a curious coincidence that experiments reached approximately the same degree of success in more than one country almost simultaneously, although everyone was working independently. There is, of course, only one theory of flight, and the laws of aero-dynamics must follow their marked-out path.

One of these inventors, however, was bound actually to fly before the rest, and it was to the Wright Brothers, working secretly in a remote part of America, that the honour finally fell. They will go down in history as the men who first flew in a heavier-than-air machine. It is significant that these two, Wilbur and Orville, are always referred to as 'the Wright Brothers,' and are given equal credit for their great achievement. They worked together in close harmony, and one did as much as the other to attain success. Actually it was Wilbur who, on a bitterly cold day, 17th December 1903, *really and truly flew.* His flight lasted only twelve seconds, and was followed by a slightly longer one by Orville. Taking it in turns, they made two more flights, the fourth one lasting 59 seconds, covering a distance of 852 feet over the ground against a twenty-mile-an-hour wind, their speed a bare 36 m.p.h. After the fourth flight, a gust of wind blew the plane over, and it had to be dismantled and taken home.

Improving on their original design, they continued their experiments until, two years later, they were able to cover a distance of 24¼ miles.

Meanwhile, the news that the Wrights had flown had filtered through to other countries, and was barely believed. Their experiments had been carried out mostly at Kitty Hawk, a place far from reporters and crowds. It was not so much secrecy that they desired as to be left in peace, but this made it difficult for them to prove their claim that they were the first men in the world to fly. Long and painful was the litigation that necessarily followed their efforts to prove it and to patent their designs. America, their own country, refused to recognise their claim, and it was Great Britain that finally came forward to give them their due.

Eventually, Orville Wright agreed to sell his patents to the British Government for the nominal sum of £15,000. They also bought the original plane, and it was given an honoured place in the South Kensington Science Museum, where it still is to-day. Meantime, Wilbur Wright had died of typhoid in 1912, worn out with the anxiety and distress the litigation had caused him.

It seems incredible that in the short space of thirty-five years the aeroplane has made such progress that speeds have gone up from 35 to nearly 500 m.p.h., distances covered non-stop from a few hundred yards to over 7000 miles, and heights from a few feet to the stratosphere, more than ten miles high. Most civilised countries are now a network of airlines, practically every town has its airport, and there are ever fewer people who still will own that they dare not fly.

Orville Wright I met in the States some four years ago. I gazed with awe and respect at this quiet, retiring, grey-haired man who was in truth the first conqueror of the air.

Rivalling him in modesty is A. V. Roe, one of the first of the English contingent to fly. A ship's engineer by trade, he began his experiments with model aircraft, basing his ideas about form and the theory of flight on sea-gulls, which he used to watch by the hour soaring in the wake of his ship. At last he succeeded in making a model which flew tolerably well, so he set to work to convert it into a man-size machine. Working at Brooklands, with no finance behind him, he encountered opposition, ridicule, and difficulties which would have deterred a less determined man. Taking no notice, he persevered. When the plane was built, he could not find an engine suitable for it, so made his first flying experiments with the machine as a glider, being towed into the air by a car. He then found a French Antoinette engine of 24 h.p. that seemed to be what he wanted. When he had fitted it into his plane, his machine flew. Only a few feet, but it was off the ground, and really airborne.

This was in June 1908, and at the same time Colonel Moore-Brabazon was also making his first flight. For many years it was an accepted fact that A. V. Roe was actually the first man to fly in England, but a Commission was set up recently to examine the rival claims of the two men, and it was decided that as Roe's flights were not officially observed, the honour must be accorded to Colonel Moore-Brabazon.

In France, Santos Dumont was the first to fly, his flight preceding A. V. Roe's by seven months. Although we cannot claim to have led the world so far as the actual practical flying was concerned, yet we should be proud of our countryman, Sir George Cayley, who worked out the science of flight a whole century before the rest of the world.

Amongst the famous names of the early pioneer days was Claude Grahame-White. With cap pulled down on his head and turned back to front, he was a well-known figure in those days of experiment and broken machines. He is one of the few who were lucky enough to make a financial success out of the beginnings of aviation. The owner of land which is now Hendon Aerodrome, he sold it to the Government just before the War for a reputed fortune.

A short time ago I saw him at Hanworth air-park, where several pilots had been invited to try out a tiny ultra-light plane with a motor-cycle engine. Those of us who were used to hundreds of horse-power to drag us through the air could not get used to the fragile thing, and we did not particularly enjoy our experience. Grahame-White, however, pulling on his cap back to front, stepped into the cockpit, took off, and flew the plane perfectly, although it was the first time he had flown since the War. His remark was: 'Why, flying hasn't changed any since my day!' Hasn't it?

No sooner had the first step been taken of actually getting machines to fly than, naturally, their inventors quickly became more ambitious and tried to fly farther afield. Also, once the miracle of flight was believed and accepted, more people came forward with the necessary finance, and newspapers began to offer big prizes for the best flights. Aviation Meetings were arranged, the first in France in 1909, when Farman (one of the best-known French pioneers) flew for 120 miles non-stop, and Blériot attained a speed of 50 m.p.h. in a flight round the course.

It was Louis Blériot who won the great honour of being the first man to cross the Channel in a heavier-than-air machine. In 1909 the *Daily Mail* offered a prize of £1000 for the first man to fly the Channel. What an incentive to those for the most part penniless inventors, quite apart from the glory! Two Frenchmen, Hubert Latham and Louis Blériot, were first in the field and were rivals for the honour. Latham was flying a little Antoinette monoplane of Voisin, which he could manage to keep in the air for an hour—enough almost to cross the Channel and back—whilst Blériot worked hard on his own design of a monoplane smaller than the Antoinette and using less power. Fitted into it was only a tiny 22 h.p. Anzani engine.

On 19th July 1909, Latham took off from Calais, but a few miles out his engine spluttered and failed, and he had to come down in the Channel, where he was rescued by a French torpedo-boat. Blériot seized his chance, and rushed to get his plane ready. At dawn on 25th July he started off, and thirty-five minutes later had landed on the English coast, with one solitary photographer to welcome him.

The next big prize was for a London to Manchester flight, for which in 1910 the *Daily Mail* offered £10,000 to the first man to complete the distance within 24 hours with not more than two stops. In these days it is difficult to imagine that such a flight was regarded as almost impossible, and the prize-money, tempting though it was, as pretty safe. Even the enthusiastic inventors themselves knew that winning would not be easy.

The two principal rivals in this race for £10,000 were Claude Grahame-White, flying a Farman plane he had bought in France, and Louis Paulhan, a Frenchman. Grahame-White had had the field to himself to begin with, and had set off one day early in April. After covering 117 miles he came down for petrol, and his machine was blown over on the ground by a sudden gust of wind, ruining his hopes for the time being. Repairs were feverishly rushed through, but in the meantime Paulhan had brought his machine across from France and was hurrying to start.

On 27th April at five o'clock in the evening, he set off. As soon as he learned his rival had gone, Grahame-White hastened to start his plane, and followed Paulhan into the air about an hour later. Unfortunately, he had lost a valuable hour of daylight and was forced to land behind Paulhan. However, so keen was he to catch up on the Frenchman that he was in the air again at 2.50 in the morning, and was only twenty miles behind when Paulhan took off at 4 o'clock from Lichfield, where he had landed the night before.

Grahame-White was unable to make up on Paulhan, who went on to win a fortune, Grahame-White sportingly giving him all the credit and praise he deserved.

The impossible was accomplished, and Lord Northcliffe racked his brains for a new impossible. £10,000 was then offered for the first flight across the Atlantic. As well say to the Moon ! How fantastic such a flight seemed in those days, and yet this far-seeing man knew that some day his prize must be won. But it was not until after the War that his promise was to be redeemed.

The War came at a time when the aeroplane was barely being taken seriously as a means of transport, far less as a powerful weapon of attack, but it did not take military technicians long to realise what possibilities the aeroplane held as an instrument of war. On the advice of experts, the Governments of all countries poured money into the aeroplane industry, and, for once, the days of stinting and contriving were over. There is no doubt that the Great War, terrible as it was for most things, was the best stimulus aviation could have had.

The War commenced only eleven years after an aeroplane flew at all, and only four years after the historic flight from London to Manchester, which had been a world sensation. Yet, within a couple of years of the outbreak of war, planes were carrying four and five men and a load of bombs at speeds up to 100 m.p.h., whilst at the end of the War in 1918, the Air Force was playing a part as important as that of any of the other fighting Services.

Engines and planes had become much more efficient and reliable and pilots more skilful, though many of the best were lost. Names like McCudden, Bishop, Ball, Mannock, René Fonck, Guynemer, and Rickenbacker will remain ever green in our memories, though almost all paid the price of their bravery.

After the War ended, there began an era in aviation which became packed with romance, adventure, and glamour—the era of long-distance record flying. Famous names and large fortunes were made overnight; newspapers splashed vivid headlines and ran startling stories of daring and endurance; aeroplanes and engines became ever more efficient and reliable as exorbitant demands were made on them. The period must be one of the most exciting and fascinating of any this usually dull old world has produced. In twenty years we almost reached the stage where we could really believe in flights to the Moon, the only deterrent being that it would be pretty cold and cheerless when we got there.

I had my fun in this exciting era, and, although one has to be glad that the days of solid, regular commercial transport have succeeded the thrilling pioneer days, I cannot help feeling a little sadness that those days are over. To me now an aeroplane is just another means of transport, and a rather monotonous one at that.

From the moment when Blériot and Latham vied with each other to be the first to cross water in an aeroplane, the spirit of friendly rivalry and competition was born. After the War the time was ripe for it to be indulged to the full in long-distance flights, altitude and speed records. There were hundreds of war machines, reliable and capable of carrying heavy loads, even if they were clumsy and ugly, which were admirable for long flights, and the pilots to man them had experience to add to their efficiency.

Moreover, it was suddenly remembered that there was a prize to be won for the first flight across the Atlantic. £10,000 and fame were awaiting the man who had the courage to take the risk. Planes were in existence which could just make the crossing, with luck and following winds, and petrol in place of bombs.

John Alcock and Arthur Whitten Brown took the chance in 1919, flying a War-time Vickers Vimy with two 350 h.p. Rolls-Royce Eagle engines. Others before them had tried and failed. So tempting a prize was bound to provoke intense rivalry and the taking of chances.

Alcock and Brown flew from Newfoundland to Ireland on 13th June 1919. The coast-to-coast crossing took them 15 hours 57 minutes. Alcock piloted and Brown navigated, so accurately that they struck the Irish coast-line only three miles off their course. Their average speed was 122½ m.p.h.

What bare statements to describe such a stupendous feat! It was almost too great to be really appreciated, and War days had made everyone used to the unexpected. Lacking as it was, too, in spectacular adventures, there was little story beyond the astounding fact that the Atlantic had been flown, and a war-worn people are hard to rouse to enthusiasm. The fliers were knighted by the King and received their reward of £10,000, but to-day how few people, except historians and pilots, remember who first flew the Atlantic.

There then broke out a veritable epidemic of long-distance flying. War pilots without jobs found this was a way in which they could use their knowledge and experience to a most profitable end, if successful, and if unsuccessful—well, it was only one more risk added to the countless ones they had been taking every day for four years.

Newspapers offered large sums for the stories of flights; the more adventures, the higher the profit. And in those days there was plenty of opportunity for adventure. Engines were always failing, pilots constantly losing their way because of inferior maps and lack of weather reports and adequate equipment, and courses taken were as often as not over barren, wild country. Newspapers found grand material for front-page stories. The lone fight of human endurance against Nature's overwhelming odds was the favourite. Setting off unknown to face the unknown, against parental opposition, with no money, friends, or influence, ran it a close second. Clichés like 'blazing trails,' flying over 'shark-infested seas,' 'battling with monsoons,' and 'forced landings amongst savage tribes' became familiar diet for breakfast.

Unknown names became household words, whilst others, those of the failures, were forgotten utterly except by kith and kin. Oceans were crossed, impenetrable jungles safely passed, and remote mountain ranges drawn intimately near. Flights to distant parts of the Empire, once proved possible, quickly became popular. Sir Alan Cobham pioneered the route to Australia and opened up Africa, until then the 'Dark Continent.' Kingsford-Smith braved the unknown dangers of the Pacific; Bert Hinkler started the race for records with his flight to Australia in 15½ days, proving not only that it was possible to get there by air, but that this could be the quickest way of doing so.

Women came into the picture when it was found that flying needed not so much physical strength as endurance, patience, and resource, all qualities possessed by women in great measure ever since the world began. Names like Lady Heath, Lady Bailey, the Duchess of Bedford, and Amelia Earhart became as familiar as those of Roe and Grahame-White.

At home the Schneider Trophy Race was held annually, until Great Britain won it outright in 1931, and speeds soared under its stimulus. Altitude records were won and lost and won again, until British engines achieved their reputation of being second to none in the world.

The Air Circus, largely through Sir Alan Cobham, came into being, and machines toured the country, taking hundreds of thousands of people up for their first ride and thrilling them with incredible manœuvres.

To-day there are still one or two sporadic record flights, an occasional plane may be seen taking people up for joy-rides, but there is no doubt that this era is over. Huge airliners, with their load of passengers and mail, are thronging the aerial roads paved by lonely pioneers.

Regular services go thrice weekly to Australia, using comfortable four-engined flying-boats, whilst your letters can go there in nine days at the cost of only 1½d. per half-ounce. Flying-boats take you three times a week to Africa and eight times a week to Egypt and India. You can fly from end to end of Europe, and will soon be able to cross every ocean.

It has become an axiom that the record flight of yesterday is the ordinary airline performance of to-day, but, although we have gone far, we have yet farther to go to realise this truth to the full. The record to Australia, for example, stands at 71 hrs. 18 secs. and belongs to Charles Scott and Tom Campbell Black, who established it in 1934. It is not beaten yet, although young Alex. Henshaw, the latest recruit to long-distance record-breaking, has his eye on it. Airline times to-day are still far from equalling this record time of yesterday, and Flying-Officer Clouston's record time of three hours under the eleven days to New Zealand and back, and Alex. Henshaw's to Cape Town of 39 hrs. 23 mins. for the outward journey, 39 hrs. 36 mins. for the homeward flight, are likely to stay as record times for some long while yet.

To-day is the era of commercial transport, when the hard work of the pioneers is being reaped in solid gain. Too rarely, unfortunately, does the man who has sown the seed reap it, but perhaps all those who were in at the start will have their reward in the remembrance of the adventures they have had, and be able to gaze, with some share of pride, at aviation as they have helped to make it.

So important is the aeroplane to-day in commerce and, alas! in war, that it is often forgotten that there can be any fun or sport in flying.

Until the Civil Air Guard scheme was inaugurated recently, the problem of expense in learning to fly was acute. Even with the coveted licence in one's possession, there still arose the serious matter of expense when a career in flying, or the ownership of a plane, was thought of as the logical sequence of learning to fly.

A career in aviation for a man is now a reasonable proposition. Training is easy, and comparatively cheap, and jobs are numerous and well-paid. Between the ages of 18 and 25, a man can join the Royal Air Force, either in a permanent capacity if he wants to stay there, or under a short service commission if he merely wants the training and experience. With that background, and a little further training according to the particular job he has in mind, he can become an airline pilot, an instructor, an air-taxi pilot, a racing pilot, record-breaker, navigator, radio operator, etc.

For a woman there is not quite the same opportunity, largely because the R.A.F. is closed to her, and there is too much traditional prejudice to allow of her being given a responsible job like that of an airline pilot. She has, however, almost as good a chance as a man to be an instructor or an air-taxi pilot—if she is good enough, whilst there are odd jobs like trailing advertisement banners, towing sail-planes, etc., for which she will probably be accepted.

For a woman the road to success is not well sign-posted, with cut-and-dried methods of training and regular jobs and regular pay waiting at the end of it. There is still prejudice to be overcome, but it is being rapidly realised that a good pilot is a good pilot, whether man or woman.

The Civil Air Guard scheme presents a wonderful opportunity to the novice wanting to learn to fly. Men and women have exactly the same chance, and the age-limit is 18 to 50. The only applicants turned down are those who fail the medical, are already enlisted in any of the fighting forces, or prove to be unsuitable as pilots after they have been given a trial lesson. It is now possible to get an 'A' licence for as low a sum as £5, everything included.

For some months I was reporting on the activities of the scheme for a well-known newspaper and so had a particularly good opportunity for studying its development in all parts of the country. It was immediately obvious that the existing equipment of Light Aeroplane Clubs could not cope with the enormous demands made upon it when thousands of people rushed to join. There was bound to be dissatisfaction amongst those who were necessarily put on the waiting-list.

In the eight months the scheme has been under operation up to the moment of writing this paragraph, several aspects of it have become clearer as time has gone on. Probably the most important is that if the main idea of the scheme is to include it as part of our National Defence programme, increased facilities for training must be given to those who prove themselves most useful for national service. The most recent ruling of the five Commissioners appointed to advise on the scheme, in conjunction with the Air Ministry, is to classify all existing and future 'A' licence holders into three broad groups:

(1) Class A to consist of men between the ages of 18 to 30 who might be eligible as Service pilots in time of war, and men of over 30 who have considerable flying experience or instructural qualifications.

(2) Class B to consist of men up to 40 years of age who would not be eligible by reason of age or on medical or other grounds for Class A, but who might be able to undertake other Service flying duties, such as observers, wireless operators, or air gunners.

(3) Class C to consist of men who do not fall into either of the above categories, and all women who might be suitable for employment as ferry pilots, ambulance pilots, or for general communication duties.

Classes A and B will have the opportunity of some further training for specially selected pilots, but Class C will receive no additional instruction—which seems a pity, as the ten hours of flying allowed annually under the Civil Air Guard at present are as good as useless from the point of view of practical usefulness in case of war.

The Civil Air Guard is a national organisation, having as its main object the training of pilots for use in war. It would seem, therefore, sounder and wiser policy to train well those with a 'flair' for flying than to waste money and time on people who will never make good pilots, even though they manage to get a licence. There has been no compulsory method of selection, and applicants have usually been taken on by the Clubs in order of application—providing, of course, they pass the medical tests. Many hundreds of potentially useful young men may thus be kicking their heels in impatience on the waiting-list. The Civil Air Guard scheme could be made into an extremely useful Reserve Force if carefully selected applicants were thoroughly trained in cross-country flying, night flying, and aerobatics, and given some elementary instruction in Service flying and discipline.

However, the matter is a highly controversial one and is even now being argued backwards and forwards in the columns of our newspapers, in the technical aviation magazines, and in the Flying Clubs themselves. It is not my purpose to discuss the pros and cons in a book of this nature. There is one indisputable fact which I can mention without fear of contradiction, and that is, that the scheme has brought new life into the Light Aeroplane Club movement, where some stimulus was badly needed, and has put such clubs on their feet again. At the moment of writing, some sixty Aero Clubs in all parts of the country are participating in the scheme, and approximately 330 aircraft are being used for training purposes. Out of some 35,000 original applicants, approximately 6000 have passed the medical tests and been in training since the inauguration of the scheme, nearly 1500 to date having obtained their 'A' licences. It is estimated that out of the above 35,000 applications, about 17,000 are suitable for training under the scheme.

Time alone will show whether the scheme is a useful one and the money well spent.

CHAPTER II

TO AUSTRALIA AND NEW ZEALAND

BRITAIN and New Zealand, the most widely separated parts of the Empire, with half the world between them, are none-the-less intimately linked by ties of kinship which have always brought them together in spirit, if not in reality. Now the aeroplane has bridged the gap between dreams and fact.

From the beginning of the Air Age it was obvious to anyone with a grain of foresight that this route would sooner or later be a main imperial trunk airline. We are bound to take advantage of each and every step in progressive transport for more closely linking up our scattered Empire. We have interests along the whole of the route—in Egypt, Palestine, Iraq, India, Burma, Malaya, Australia, and New Zealand—and a child can see that if the air provides the fastest method of transport, then air transport must be utilised to the full.

In the early years, however, only the very few aviation loyalists had faith that such an ideal would ever be achieved, and even they, no matter how enthusiastic they were, hardly visualised the present-day schedules as they are. But the steps forward have been so rapid that to-day almost anything will be believed of the future. You have only to say: 'Well, look what has already been achieved in thirty-six years.' (The first aeroplane flight was made late in 1903.) 'In another fifty, at this rate of progress, why shouldn't we have attained speeds of a thousand miles an hour, or even more, and in a hundred years, who can say that we may not fly to the Moon?'

The long route to New Zealand via Australia has been built up by degrees. It has been extended gradually from an England–Egypt airline to an England–India; then England–Australia; and now England–New Zealand.

First, a number of small airline companies operated between London and Paris—the first link in the long chain. Next, the Royal Air Force ran experimental services over 1100 miles between Cairo and Basra via Baghdad. It may seem strange that the Air Force should do this, but it must be remembered that after the War almost all our aeroplanes were military, War pilots had the most experience, and it was necessary to find some use for them. This was easy so far as it concerned those squadrons that found themselves after the War in Egypt, Palestine, and Iraq. Great Britain had the task of restoring order over a great part of the Middle East, and it was vital for Palestine and Iraq to be patrolled. In 1921 a conference was held in Cairo at which it was decided to use aeroplanes for transport, instead of constructing a most expensive railway, as had been suggested. At that time it was recognised that ultimately a route must go through to Australia, and this seemed a good opportunity to pioneer part of the line and train pilots in long-distance flying.

Previous to this decision, however, in 1919 two Australians, Keith and Ross Smith (later knighted for their achievement), actually flew the whole way to Australia, being the first to do so. The Australian Government had offered a prize of £10,000 to the first Australian pilot to complete a flight from England to Australia within thirty days, in a British aeroplane. The Vickers Aircraft Company took up the challenge, chose as aeroplane the Vickers-Vimy, as flown by Alcock and Brown on their flight across the Atlantic, and for pilot Ross Smith, with Keith Smith, his brother, as navigator, and two sergeants as mechanics.

The route was selected by the Air Ministry, and naturally took the shortest way consistent with the existing aerodromes, air routes, and British territory. It lay via Cairo, Karachi, Calcutta, Singapore, and Port Darwin—a total distance of 11,294 miles as planned by the Air Ministry. Actually, Ross Smith gained time often by taking short-cuts, and made a saving of 470 miles.

This route is by no means the shortest to Australia, but, with slight modifications, it has remained the airline in use till this day. Unfortunately, for reasons geographical, political, and commercial, it is not at present possible to choose any other route, although theoretically, once in the air, terrestrial barriers lose almost the whole of their significance.

The earth being a sphere, the shortest possible distance between any two points is therefore part of a circle. If you take a globe of the world and draw a piece of string across from London to Sydney, you will see that it cuts through Moscow, Southern Russia, and the Caucasus, right across Tibet, with its almost impassable mountain ranges, down through part of China just to the south of Hong Kong, over the China Seas to Borneo, and thence across the Timor Sea to Port Darwin and on to Sydney over the Australian Desert.

Such a route would cut some thousand miles off the route used at present, but it is obvious that this line has nothing whatever to offer but speed. It will probably be used at some near future date for the purpose of record-breaking, so soon as an aeroplane is built which has speed sufficient to break the existing record of just under three days set up by Scott and Campbell Black in 1934, plus a range which will cover the ground between the few aerodromes on the route, plus also enough performance to clear the mountains of Tibet, rising to heights of over 20,000 feet. Commercially, the route is useless, as there is not enough traffic *en route* to make it worth while.

The course chosen for the Smiths' flight was the logical one, although the first stage from London to Cairo was by no means All-Red, and permits had to be obtained from numerous foreign Governments. The subsequent history of the route shows that again and again it had to be changed because of lack of agreement with certain of the countries in which landings were necessary. At one time even part of the journey had to be done by train. To-day, the policy of using flying-boats has made it possible to plan a route where we alight only in British waters and harbours, or in harbours controlled by us.

Ross Smith chose to fly from London to Lyons, thence via Pisa, Rome, Taranto, and Crete to Cairo—a total distance of 2285 miles. The second stage was via Damascus, Ramadi, Basra, and Bandar

Abbas in Persia to Karachi, a distance of 2580 miles. All these places boasted aerodromes, most of them military, and Ross Smith had already flown over this route in 1918, carrying Major-General Geoffrey Salmond on a diplomatic mission.

The third stage, from Karachi to Calcutta—the route is obvious—goes straight across India to Calcutta, and Air Force landing grounds could be used. Ross Smith landed at Delhi to refuel. Stage 4, Calcutta to Singapore, involves a long sea crossing if a direct route is taken. To avoid this, a route was chosen by way of Akyab, Rangoon, Bangkok, and the east coast of the Malay Peninsula to Singapore. On this stage ground organisation was practically non-existent, and landings had to be made on race-courses or in fields. The final stage, from Singapore to Port Darwin, crossed some of the islands of the Dutch East Indies, where the Governor-General courteously had prepared landing grounds for the fliers. At Batavia there was a landing ground used by the Royal Dutch Air Force, but beyond that lay 1710 miles before Port Darwin was reached without so much as a single aerodrome or emergency ground of any description. Moreover, in country where dense jungle was the rule, the difficulty of making and keeping clear any large enough piece of ground was enormous. An alternative route from Singapore, using British territory via Borneo, New Guinea, and Thursday Island, has never been tried out, although it was suggested at the time of Ross Smith's flight. It is slightly longer, and involves a considerable amount of sea crossing, which, in those days of less reliable engines, was a factor of great importance.

The preparations for this first through flight to Australia must have been formidable. Where Air Force aerodromes were already in being it was fairly simple, as supplies of petrol and oil, spare parts, and mechanics would be on the spot. Once beyond Calcutta, however, with the exception of one or two grounds in the Dutch East Indies, no organisation of any sort existed. Casks of petrol and oil had to be shipped out, landing grounds chosen and prepared, permits requested for flying into and over foreign territories, maps collected and marked with flying data, long-distance petrol-tanks made for the machine, etc., etc. No flight of such magnitude had ever been attempted before, and no one knew the ropes. It remained for Ross and Keith Smith to find things out for themselves.

Rather than try to tell you of the difficulties they had to encounter, of which I have only read, I will recount to you a little later some of my own adventures over the same route, which may give you some slight idea of the kind of troubles the early fliers had to face, even though my own way was made smooth by the flights of the Smith Brothers, Sir Alan Cobham, Bert Hinkler, and others.

Ross and Keith Smith left Hounslow, at that time the civil air-port of London, on 12th November 1919, and, after a flight in which they met with almost every sort of weather and climate and every imaginable difficulty, they succeeded in reaching Australia on 10th December—27 days 20 hours after leaving London—to win £10,000 and be knighted for their history-making flight. Now Australia has been reached in under three days, but nothing can take away from the Smiths that they were the first.

Naturally enough, many other flights followed, the one after Ross Smith's taking seven months, which gives some indication of just how marvellous was the first flight of less than a month. In fact, Ross Smith's 'record' stood until 1928, when Bert Hinkler flew to Australia in the then astounding time of 15½ days.

No one tried to bring down Ross Smith's time until in 1926 Alan Cobham set out for Australia and back in a seaplane with the expressed intention of making as fast time as he could. He wanted to explore the possibilities of making the route into an airline, and his theory was that flying-boats should be used rather than landplanes, and also that, as far as practicable, British territory should be crossed rather than foreign. He set off in June 1926 in a D.H. 50 seaplane fitted with an Armstrong-Siddeley Jaguar engine, which gave him no trouble the whole of the flight—something very unusual in those early days. Cobham was very thorough in his organisation, and was of a nature specially suited to carrying through the intricate, lengthy, and difficult preliminary arrangements which a flight then necessarily involved. It took him 39 days to reach Port Darwin, and although he followed practically the same route as Ross Smith, yet, using a seaplane, he had, of course, to land on harbours and rivers instead of on aerodromes and race-courses. After the flight, he gave as his opinion that the first part of the route from England to Egypt and thence to Calcutta should be flown by landplanes, and the section from India to Australia by flying-boats.

The return journey took him 27 days along practically the same route, at the end of which he made his memorable landing on the Thames outside the Houses of Parliament—an ending ideal in theory, but one which has not been officially encouraged, owing principally to the difficulty of keeping the waterway clear. It seems a pity that our airlines to-day cannot deposit us at our front doors like this.

After Cobham came Captain Lancaster with Mrs Keith Miller, who took six months for the flight, but who were the first to do it in a light aeroplane. They reached Port Darwin in March 1928, but just before they arrived Bert Hinkler set out in the same type of machine, an Avro-Avian, single-engined, two-seater biplane of some hundred horse-power, and deliberately gave himself the task of flying to Australia as fast as he possibly could. His time of 15½ days was amazing considering the plane he used, which cruised at only 87 miles an hour, and the difficulties he had to encounter on the route. To date, this was the fastest time that had been made to Australia. It was also the longest flight so far made solo in a light aeroplane on any route, and might be called the real beginning of long-distance *record* flying.

In 1929 Flight-Lieutenant Moir and Flying-Officer Owen successfully flew to Australia in a Vickers-Vellore machine, following on their unsuccessful attempt to fly in the opposite direction. It was left to Kingsford-Smith and Ulm to make the first fast flight from Australia to England, which they completed in June/July 1929, in their famous three-engined Fokker machine, the *Southern Cross.* Francis Chichester then flew from Croydon to Port Darwin in a D.H. Gipsy Moth between 20th December 1929 and 25th January 1930.

After this comes my own flight, which I started on 5th May 1930, arriving in Australia 19½ days later. From this flight I will give you just a few of the high-lights to show what kind of difficulties we were up against in those days. Why I wanted to fly this particular route I really do not know, except that it was the greatest distance I could fly with a Gipsy Moth. Anything beyond that involved sea crossings for which I had not the range. Moreover, perhaps the route had a certain fascination, a glamour that attracted me. I was told hair-raising stories of torture-loving bandits in the mountain fastnesses of Turkey and Iraq, of wild beasts in the desert and jungle, of cannibals in the farther islands of the East Indies, and of sharks in the Timor Sea. My vivid, almost school-girl imagination was fired. Fed as I had been since childhood on fairy-tales, stories of the Arabian Nights, Greek and Northern Mythology, and innumerable books of adventure of the Rider Haggard and Jules Verne type, it was no wonder that the dangers frightened but enchanted me. Difficulties technical, financial, and parental had no power to stop me once my mind was made up, and I rode somewhat rough-shod over bunches of red tape, with the help and encouragement of Sir Sefton Brancker, then Director of Civil Aviation and responsible for obtaining Lord Wakefield's invaluable financial help for the flight.

So far as preparations went, I was faced by a complete and utter ignorance on the part of myself and everybody else. The first person I found to give me any advice at all of a helpful nature was Captain Hope, from whom I bought my machine, a second-hand Gipsy Moth which had already flown some 35,000 miles, mostly carrying pictures which Hope was bringing home for the newspapers. It was he who told me what sort of equipment I should need, where to go for maps, and added some valuable information regarding aerodromes, weather, etc.

Besides Captain Hope, the only other persons who were able to help me were Jack Humphreys, the chief engineer at the London Aeroplane Club, and Mitchell, his able second-in-command. Together they put me through my engineer's licences and taught me all I ever knew about an engine. They advised me what spares to take, and what to do when things went wrong with the engine or plane; but for their training I could never have got through.

For maps I had to take whatever I could obtain—some good, some bad. Courses and distances were marked out for me, all available aerodromes, landing grounds, and race-courses indicated, and the maps cut into strips and put on to rather clumsy 'rollers' so that I could unroll them bit by bit as I continued my course. (In theory ideal, but in practice I found they would roll backwards!) Once in possession of a list of aerodromes, I set to work to plan my route. I laid out the routes taken by previous fliers and decided on at least one innovation. It seemed to me a sheer waste of time to go such a long way round via Lyons, Rome, Cairo, Damascus, and so on to the Persian Gulf, the route flown by Ross Smith, or by way of Rome, Malta, and Ramleh, that chosen by Hinkler. From the map it appeared quite obvious that any time I could save must be on the first part of the route, as, after the Persian Gulf, one was almost bound to go the stereotyped route taken by the rest, across India, down through the Malay Peninsula, and through the Dutch East Indies to Port Darwin. I drew a line from London to Basra on the curve of the Gulf, and discovered it took me through about a dozen European countries, right across the dreaded Taurus

Mountains (about which such terrible stories were told by Air Force pilots of being held to ransom by bandits if captured), and through the Arabian Desert to Aleppo and Baghdad. The prospect did not frighten me, because I was so appallingly ignorant that I never realised in the least what I had taken on, in spite of what I was told and all the awful warnings I received. I decided to take this route. I was not concerned with political or commercial questions, and only thought of saving time so that I could beat Hinkler's record.

The first thing I was up against was permits. I found I had to give six weeks' notice and a deposit of £50 to the Air Ministry to cover expenses of cables, etc. I was also told that it was most unlikely Turkey would give me permission, and as an actual fact this permit had not arrived when I finally left on my flight. The assorted array of documents I eventually collected was something amazing to behold, including a message to the bandits asking them to guard me safely, as ransom would be paid. (I do not remember how much was promised. Certainly, however, much more than I was worth at the beginning of my flight!)

The next thing was arranging for supplies of petrol and oil. Most of it had to be shipped out specially, although on Air Force aerodromes supplies were available. In some places were unused casks from other flights.

Equipment of the machine was easy, as I had had the good fortune to buy a plane with long-distance tanks already fitted. These gave me a range of 1150 miles, or 13½ hours' flying in still air at my cruising speed of 85 m.p.h. For instruments I had an air-speed indicator, an altimeter, a turn-and-bank indicator, and one single compass. In a modern long-range aeroplane there are almost a hundred dials, knobs, and throttles! The front cockpit (my Gipsy Moth was a two-seater open biplane with one hundred-horse-power engine) was covered over, and into it I crammed a medley of tools and kit reminding me of a village store. Besides a goodly supply of tools and spares there were tyres, inner tubes, clothes, sun-helmet, mosquito-net, cooking-stove, billy-cans, synthetic fuel, flints, revolver, medicines, first-aid kit, air-cushion, and Heaven knows what else. Everything, in short, that might come in useful in the event of a forced landing, and I had to legislate for deserts, jungles or seas, mountain-tops or swamps, heat or cold, day or night. Fastened with rope to the side of the machine was a spare propeller, on the seat of my cockpit was a parachute, and in every available corner were emergency provisions. It was the only way—like taking out an umbrella every day so that it will not rain.

It took me nearly six months to prepare for the flight, and even then I left without my Turkish permit, and with last-minute news that my supplies of petrol for Timor would only be through in another two months. Time was getting short. No one knew very much about the weather conditions I should find, and when I went to the Air Ministry to make inquiries I was shown into the room where records were kept and told to help myself to any information I could discover in them. I had a vague idea that monsoons occurred during the summer months, and I read somewhere that the monsoon storms broke in the middle of May—but I never found out where (until I started !).

The day I actually set off—5th May 1930—I was aiming for Vienna, 800 miles away, and available reports gave me the weather only as far as Paris. After that I had to take what came. At Vienna there was an excellent aerodrome, with mechanics to do all the work for me, and except for the inconveniences of pumping all my petrol by means of an old-fashioned hand-pump, sitting in the discomfort of an open machine on a hard parachute for ten hours, instead of the four in which this ‘ hop ’ could be done nowadays, being without weather reports, and knowing the whole time that if anything went wrong with my engine—more than likely—I must come down where I could, this first day's flight did not differ greatly from what it might be to-day.

It was at Constantinople that I had my first taste of such ignorance on the part of several willing enough helpers that, when lifting the tail of my plane to wheel her into the hangar, they did so with far too much gusto and landed her on her nose! Fortunately, no damage was done.

I have often had arguments as to which is the greater strain—to fly through a long period at slow speeds, stopping for a night's rest every now and then, or to rush straight through, flying day and night practically without sleep. I have had both experiences and unhesitatingly say that the former is more tiring by far—at any rate, for my temperament. On my first Australian flight, after taking more than twice as long to cover any distance as it would take to-day, in an open cockpit, which is fatiguing because of the noise (we always had stub exhausts to try to increase speed and also to enable us to see the accuracy of the petrol mixture at a glance) and exposure to the weather, I had to spend hours on the ground looking after my engine, because at very few places were there trained mechanics, and it was vital to carry through a certain amount of maintenance work at the end of every day's flight. For 19½ days I had an average of only three hours' sleep per night, whilst on my last flight to the Cape I had only three hours' sleep during three and a half days. On the last Cape flight I never touched my engine except to fill with petrol and change the oil occasionally, whereas on the flight to Australia I did at least three hours' work at the end of every ten hours' flying.

In Turkey I was held up for hours owing to my permit not having been received, and it was only after a great deal of difficulty that I was allowed to proceed. Once away, I met storms and bad weather in the Taurus Mountains, of which I had no knowledge beforehand, as I never had another weather report except at the better-equipped Air Force aerodromes, and even then merely local conditions were given.

Persia demanded a health certificate, and only let me proceed without one when I pointed out that I should be out of their country in a few hours without again touching ground, and therefore I had not much chance to spread any strange and wonderful diseases, supposing I had them. They had never thought of that point of view, and let me go.

Where aerodromes did not exist I had to land on

race-courses or prepared grounds. At Rangoon, whilst searching for the race-course in a tropical downpour, I mistook for it the playing fields of an Engineering College at Insein, just outside the city. Landing in a space far too small for my plane, I ran into the ditch and did a considerable amount of damage. In this country it would have meant major repairs—new wings, blue prints by the bundle, weeks of hard work, and quite a lot of money. Having none of these at Insein, we set to work to do the best we could. Wings were patched with men's linen shirts ; new ribs, bolts, and struts were made for me by pupils of the Engineering Institute (what better place could I have chosen !) ; and dope and paint for the wings were mixed up by the local chemist.

In the Dutch East Indies, where I landed in a field in which someone had planted long pointed stakes to mark out the design for a new house, the tears in the wing fabric that resulted from landing in their midst were patched up with pink sticking-plaster.

Petrol-pumps, of course, had never been heard of in the out-of-the-way places where I wanted to refuel. The task of filling the tanks from huge casks was hard work indeed, mostly carried out in broiling heat, driving sand, or pouring rain.

And so I could go on ; but I would not have you think that those early days were without their good side too. Everywhere I went an aeroplane was a novelty, something to be gazed at with awe and admiration. In India, for example, my unexpected landing was said to have prevented a native rebellion, as it was superstitiously believed the gods had intervened. Nowadays, I am afraid, record-breaking pilots are just a nuisance, something that disorganises the routine work of airports. Although conditions to-day are what we have all ostensibly been trying to achieve, yet I myself have to admit that I am sorry the bad old days are gone.

My flight was followed by countless others. Kingsford-Smith was the first to beat Hinkler's record. In October 1930 he left Heston, reaching Port Darwin 9 days 21 hours 40 minutes later. Many tried, but failed, to beat that record, but finally Charles Scott, in April 1931, cut 17 hours off 'Smithy's' time. The record was reduced gradually during the next three years, sometimes by a few hours, sometimes by a whole day, until in October 1934 Charles Scott and Tom Campbell Black in their De Havilland Comet smashed the record to pieces by their magnificent flight of 71 hours 18 seconds. This record stands to this day, and it was not beaten even by Flying-Officer

Clouston in his recent dash to New Zealand and back, although he put up many other records, including those for the outward trip from England to New Zealand and for the round trip. To New Zealand and back, 26,000 miles, in 11 days! It is almost unbelievable.

To-day, both Imperial Airways and the Royal Netherlands Line of K.L.M. operate the route to Australia. Schedules and stopping-places are changing so frequently that, were I to set out to-day's exact time-table, the information would be past history by the time this book is published. I will therefore content myself with brief references to some of the more interesting country you will fly over, whether you take the British or Dutch line or fly to-day or to-morrow.

Across Europe K.L.M. have a winter and a summer route, the latter by way of Central Europe, from Amsterdam to Athens on a line as straight as the crow flies, the winter route avoiding the mountainous country by taking a course to Marseilles through the Rhone Valley, and thence to Rome and Athens.

Imperial Airways fly direct to Athens in flying-boats, and thence alongside K.L.M.'s line across the Mediterranean to Alexandria, important air-junction where many airways divide, some to fly to Australia and the Far East, others to South, East, and West Africa.

The route across Turkey and the Taurus Mountains which I followed is not used to-day for the Australia airway, although it is shorter in actual distance than the Mediterranean route. This is partly due to geographical, partly to political, barriers.

From Alexandria the route is over the Holy Land, evoking many a memory of some wonderful Biblical story, past Bethlehem, Jerusalem, the Dead Sea, the River Jordan, and over desolate mountains into the arid regions of Iraq.

Part of the route to romantic Baghdad parallels the enormous pipe line which carries oil from the oilfields of Iraq to the Levant. Although the terrain below is seamed with caravan trails and steeped in ancient history, yet it needs much imagination to decorate this desolate stretch with the glory of Babylon and Nineveh and to place the Garden of Eden near to sun-scorched Basra itself. It is said that in the thirteenth century Hulagu Khan and his fierce Mongol tribes destroyed the irrigation system which gave life and beauty to sand and bare rock.

Basra to-day has a very up-to-date airport, one of the few equipped for night-flying. The airway then continues over the translucent waters of the

Persian Gulf to Jask and thence to Karachi, the air gateway into India.

Across India the route is by way of Jodhpur, with its ancient temples beside one of the most modern airports in the world, to Allahabad, over country well watered by the sacred River Ganges, and on to Calcutta beside the Ganges Delta, incredibly dirty, sluggish, and choked with slimy swamps, yet none the less holy.

Between India and Burma is the Bay of Bengal, then forest-clad mountains, often hidden in mists of rain, are crossed to reach Rangoon, unmistakably signposted by the most famous of all Buddhist pagodas, the gold-encrusted Shwe Dagon dominating the entire delta plain from its eminence on the temple hill.

Jungle-smothered mountains separate Burma from Siam, a country of innumerable paddy-fields, so much water that it looks from the air like a flooded land, and villages are perched on piles or pontoons. Bangkok, the capital, is often called 'the Venice of the East.' From the air it looks like some fairy city, treble-walled, with golden pagodas flashing in the sunlight, and gold and white palaces and dazzlingly gorgeous temples looking like Christmas-tree decorations in their leafy green parks.

Over the Malay Peninsula the long airway pushes

on to Singapore, its site of great strategic importance easily appreciable from the air. Sumatra leads to Batavia, K.L.M.'s terminal before their line was extended to Australia.

Sumatra, Java, Bali, Celebes. The names of these islands of the Dutch East Indies spell music, romance, and beauty in plenty, but Timor, just beyond, is sure to conjure up visions of sharks to every avid reader of record flights. However, to-day the Timor Sea is crossed in about three hours, and though many a tale is told of these greedy fish, yet never yet has a passenger been gobbled up!

Beyond the Timor Sea lies Darwin, the North-West gate to Australia.

Imperial Airways, criticised as they have often been, have nevertheless done their share to make this wonderful airway what it is to-day. In 1924 they were given the task by the British Government of developing British commercial air transport on an economic basis. On the 26th April 1924 they began a daily London–Paris service. In 1925 a party representing the Air Ministry and Imperial Airways surveyed the Cairo–Karachi route, and in December 1926 a fortnightly Cairo to Basra mail-and-passenger service was opened, timed to connect with the P. & O. mail-boat service, Marseilles–Port Said. This was the first stage of the through

England–India service. The extension from Basra to Karachi was held up because of diplomatic difficulties with the Persian Government. (It was to try to clarify the situation in Persia that Sir Sefton Brancker left in 1930 on the R. 101, in which he lost his life.)

It was not until 1929 that London and India were joined by a passenger-carrying airline. A weekly service was started in March 1929, but the Basle–Genoa section was by rail because of diplomatic difficulties in south-eastern Europe. The European section of the route was frequently altered. In December the India service, operated by the Government of India, was extended to Jodhpur, and thence to Delhi. By April 1930 the service from England to India was accelerated to 6½ days, and in 1931 it was extended experimentally to Australia, the mail being picked up at Kupang by Kingsford-Smith and carried by the service of 'Qantas' (the main Australian airline company) to Melbourne. In April 1935 the through route from London to Brisbane and return was opened for passengers.

From that day to this it has been a story of cutting down the time, increasing the number of services run, and improving comfort for passengers. To-day experimental flights are in course of progress to extend the route to New Zealand; thrice-weekly services are run between England and Australia, and, most significant of all, the policy of using flying-boats instead of landplanes has been almost universally adopted on our Empire air routes. It is interesting to note that Sir Alan Cobham advocated this twelve years ago. On the Australia route Empire flying-boats are used between Southampton and Singapore, the rest of the journey at present being operated by 4-engined landplanes, but arrangements are being made to use flying-boats on the whole route in the near future, also for an extension to New Zealand.

At the moment Imperial Airways schedules take two days from Southampton to Basra; 9 days 2¼ hours from Southampton to Sydney and 9 days 14¼ hours for the reverse trip. The flying-boats leave Southampton every Wednesday, Saturday, and Sunday.

It is essential to speed up and increase the number of services. If it is possible to fly to Australia in under three days, as the record-breakers have shown, then it ought to be feasible for a commercial airline to do it comfortably in seven days. In any event, even now the mail could go through more quickly, but the policy of our airlines has always been to carry mails along with passengers. In America the exact contrary principle was adopted.

The only way to bring Australia within really quick reach of England is to use long-distance, high-speed planes flying day and night. The difficulties involved in achieving this ideal are great, but they will be conquered one day. The experimental flights which are being made across the North Atlantic should help materially to further the construction of a fast machine capable of long range and *able to carry a payload*, one of the most important of the factors that have always made it possible for record-breaking pilots to make airline schedules seem slow, for their entire 'payload' consists of petrol.

I think it is not too optimistic to forecast that England and Australia will be only three days apart in ten years' time.

An interesting new route via the Indian Ocean called the 'Empire Reserve Route' is at present being surveyed.

The survey is the idea of Captain P. G. Taylor—Kingsford-Smith's navigator on his second Pacific flight in 1934, and to-day one of the best-known figures in Australian aviation. The flight is being made in an American flying-boat, the *Guba*, lent by its owner, Richard Archbold, an American multi-millionaire who is making this survey flight as part of a flight around the world, and is himself taking part in it.

The *Guba* has a non-stop range of 4000 miles and is equipped with the best of everything that money can buy, including an automatic pilot to fly the plane, and the most powerful radio set yet installed on any aircraft in the world (or so the owner claims).

The proposed route is straight across the Indian Ocean to East Africa. The actual stages of the survey flight are: Port Headland in Western Australia to Cocos Island, 1200 miles; Cocos to Diego Garcia, 1470 miles (whence another projected line could extend to Ceylon); Diego Garcia to the Seychelles, 990 miles; Seychelles to Mombasa, 840 miles.[1]

The great advantage of such a route between Australia and Africa and thence to England is that if there is trouble in the Far East we have a reserve route all ready for operation. It is shorter than the overland route and could be used even now for fast mail carrying. If adopted, we shall be able to add to the world's vast network of airlines a line across the Indian Ocean, the only ocean not yet crossed by aircraft.

Later in the year it is hoped to extend the England–Australia airway to New Zealand. Survey flights have already been made.

[1] Distances as calculated by the *Aeroplane* in statute miles along the rhumb-line tracks.

Chapter III

TO CAPE TOWN VIA CAIRO

This route I have flown only once, from Cape Town to London, as compared with three times via the west coast and across the Sahara. I am afraid I should not have flown it even this once had I not been compelled reluctantly to change my plans at the last minute for the return journey of my latest Cape flight, in May 1936.

One or two of the aerodromes I had chosen along the west coast of Africa were in such a neglected state owing to disuse that I dared not repeat the dangerous heavy-load take-offs I had just managed to survive on the way out. I had tanks in my plane capable of holding enough fuel for two thousand miles non-stop flying, but to take off with such a load needed a good level surface of a thousand yards length at the very least. The aerodromes of the Belgian line Sabena and of Air France were off my route (although on one hop I made a detour so that I could take off from Cotonou, where the runway was of the length I required), and once I had left the excellent French military aerodromes in

Morocco and the Sahara, I had nothing suitable till Cape Town was reached. I decided that discretion was the better part of valour, and that I would go home via an orthodox air route.

It was my first experience of traversing an organised air route, and, whilst I appreciated the many blessings it provided, yet I did not particularly enjoy the experience. I could not quite shake off the feeling that I was a trespasser, and a nuisance at that. For the first time on any long-distance flight I found that an aeroplane was no novelty, and that if I wanted anything done I had usually to do it myself—and pay for it! Nothing could have demonstrated to me more clearly that flying is now a commonplace than to find comfortable hotels along the route, where I was charged to the hilt for my flask of coffee, packet of sandwiches, or cold drinks on landing.

Before I left England it took me over two months to organise the flight via the Sahara, but the return plans were made at Cape Town during a Sunday afternoon. Three cables obtained the necessary permits for the Sudan, Tripoli, and Greece (my knowing General Balbo and His Majesty the King of Greece materially helped, no doubt); maps were borrowed, petrol and oil were to be found everywhere, and there was nothing else to do except set off, which I did after a couple of days' rest.

I cannot claim to have done anything on this flight that countless others had not already done before me. I cut down the record time by a small margin, knowing full well that the new record could not stand for long. It was, indeed, broken by Flying-Officer Clouston in November 1937, when he flew the same route in 45 hours 2 minutes, returning in 57 hours 23 minutes, with a total elapsed time, including halt for rest in Cape Town, of 5 days 17 hours 28 minutes for the round trip. A short time ago, even this magnificent record was broken by Henshaw, flying a Percival Mew Gull, tiny racing monoplane, who lowered Clouston's time by 39 hours, taking, however, the shorter but more difficult Sahara route.

This is what flying has come to now. South Africa and back within four days! It is not much more than half a century ago that maps of the Dark Continent showed little except isolated settlements on the coast-line and a white blank for the unexplored interior. It was only in 1858 that Lake Tanganyika, to-day skirted by huge airliners, was discovered, and not till later that the Nile, now giving harbourage for flying-boats, was traced to its source. The great ambition of Cecil Rhodes was an 'All-Red' railway route from Cairo to the Cape. That dream is even yet unfulfilled, but the 'All-Red' route by air is now a reality.

Alexandria is to-day the great junction from which branch off our longest airlines. For two thousand years the greatest port in the Near East, the Air Age finds Alexandria the greatest aerial gateway to Egypt and Africa. Imperial Airways use flying-boats for both routes as far as Alexandria. One branch then goes east to India and Australia, that branching in its turn at Bangkok for Hong Kong, whilst the other turns south for Cairo and Durban. Flying-boats are now used on the African route to Durban. Kisumu is the junction where a change-over can be made to a land plane if Johannesburg, Cape Town, or some inland town is the destination. Thrice-weekly services leave Southampton for Durban every Wednesday, Friday, and Saturday, making the journey in 4½ days.

It was in 1918 that the first survey by air was made over the ground separating Cairo from Cape Town in order to decide which route an airline should follow. It is not always practicable, unfortunately, to take the obvious 'bee-line.' Sometimes natural barriers stand in the way, sometimes political, and often enough it is the lack of commerce *en route*. As someone neatly put it: 'We may take it as an axiom that a world route follows the line of least resistance and greatest profit.' Information was needed with regard to climatic, transport, and flying conditions, and aerodromes had to be chosen and prepared. This last was found to be one of the most difficult tasks of all. In some places it was necessary to cut them out of dense jungle. Thousands of trees and shrubs had to be felled and dug up by their roots, whilst innumerable ant-hills had to be levelled. It is said that 'at N'dola, where 700 natives were working from April to August, 25,000 tons (of earth from ant-hills) were removed from the ground cleared.'

The most difficult part of the whole route, so far as making aerodromes was concerned, was the central section, where most of the ground was covered with dense brush and tropical forest. It needed almost as much labour to keep the ground cleared as it took to get it clear in the first place, because, in those parts of the world, vegetation grows so quickly and luxuriantly that if a clearing is neglected for only a few weeks, it ceases to be distinguishable from the forest from which it was snatched. In between landing grounds it would have been impossible to effect a landing safely. Add to this the difficulties of land transport, and the facts that no oxen could be used because of the prevalence of the tsetse-fly, that water was scarce, and that mosquitoes and white ants swarmed, and some of the obstacles may be understood.

Even now this middle section of the route is distinctly unpleasant to fly over. Rain falls all the year round, and thunder-storms are the order of the day. They arise almost without warning, and are particularly violent. I shall never forget skirting one rather closely just before reaching Juba. Enormous lumps of black clouds seemed to have some sort of magnetic power, because I could feel myself being literally drawn in towards them. The sheets of rain even on the fringe of the storm seem to smother you and bear you down, and I believe it would be quite impossible to fly right through the deluge at its centre. During the day it is easy enough to thread your way through the thinnest of the rains, but at night it is much more difficult to distinguish between flyable and impassable weather. Beaten down by a cloud-burst, you peer this way and that amongst shades of blackness, lit every now and then by piercing streaks of lightning which only serve to show up a steaming sea of tree-tops rising and falling with the unevenness of the land, for all the world like a black choppy sea. I have tried many a time to climb up over the storms, but at 15,000 feet have seen cloudy

Himalayas stretching seemingly without summit into the dark sky.

The northern section, from Cairo along the Nile Valley, was comparatively simple so far as choice of route, ground transport, and the making of aerodromes were concerned. It was found on the survey flight that landings could be made in many places other than the prepared landing grounds. From Cairo to Khartoum the ground is desert, with the Nile winding between sand-banks, on which landings could easily be effected if necessary. From Cairo the Nile was followed as far as Wadi Halfa, then the railway, until the Nile was picked up again farther on and followed to Khartoum. From Khartoum a line was taken across the Sudd, and then almost due south to Uganda.

Weather over this section is usually good, but dust-storms are frequent, making visibility very difficult. On my own flight, trying to follow the railway was much harder than would have been a direct compass course. Ahead I could see nothing, whilst the view directly below was hidden by my wings. The only way I kept the railway in sight was by glancing behind from time to time, and, had I once lost it, I should never have been able to find it again. This is not so important these days, when planes have enough range to cross the desert non-stop, but in the early days, when landings had to be made for refuelling on an aerodrome beside the railway, it would have been a tragic disaster to miss it.

On the southern section, across Rhodesia to the Zambesi River and thence to Bulawayo and along the railway to Pretoria, Johannesburg, and Cape Town, conditions were found to be very much more favourable. Ground communications were generally far better, as the southern part of Africa is much more developed. Even so, there were long stretches of bush country and rolling plains without any habitation except native villages, and before Cape Town was reached the mountains of South Africa had to be crossed. Johannesburg is 6000 feet above sea-level, and most of the other landing grounds from Khartoum southwards are on the same plateau, so that high-altitude take-offs and landings had to be catered for.

The expedition was planned with great care and much information was gained. Before it set off, the meteorologist who had been going into weather conditions had advised: 'The best time for a pioneer flight is between December and March. Later on, unless the ground organisation, which must include weather reports and rapid communications, becomes much more elaborate, flying in Central Africa is almost impossible.' We have certainly gone a long way since then!

A Vickers-Vimy was tanked up to give a range of 1000 miles, Lord Northcliffe nobly stepped forward to finance the flight, and Doctor Chalmers Mitchell, a member of the *Times* Staff and for many years Secretary of the Zoological Society, was put in charge. Two pilots, a mechanic, and a rigger made up the crew. In spite of the tremendous amount of care that was put into the preliminary preparations, nothing but misfortune attended this flight. Finally the Vimy crashed at Tabora, having flown 2662 miles in 21 days.

In the meantime another Vickers-Vimy plane had been purchased by the South African Government to make a similar attempt to fly from London to Cape Town. Its pilots, two South African officers, Lieut.-Colonel Van Ryneveld and Flight-Lieutenant Brand, eventually succeeded in reaching Cape Town, but only after they had crashed at Bulawayo, finishing the journey in a machine sent to them by the Government of South Africa.

Most of the mishaps on both these flights could be attributed, firstly, to inadequate ground organisation and incomplete survey of the route and, secondly, to engine troubles arising out of the extreme climatic conditions encountered, conditions with which existing engines were not built to cope.

After these two experimental flights, and two other abortive attempts, no further development was made until, in 1926, Sir Alan Cobham decided to try out the possibilities of the route. He chose a De Havilland D.H. 50 machine and took with him a cinematographer and a mechanic. As usual, he left nothing to chance before taking off on the flight, and spent many months in preliminary organisation. Landing grounds had to be prepared, supplies of fuel sent out, and hosts of officials dealt with. His flight was uneventful, except for the usual difficulties of blinding storms hampering visibility and swamping aerodromes, making heavy-load take-offs a most dangerous matter. The day had already been reached when aeroplanes and engines were sufficiently reliable to make this an axiom : So long as you are up in the air you are safe, but what goes up must sooner or later come down, and then the trouble starts.

Over the desert near Atbara Cobham was lost in a sandstorm ; at N'dola the sodden ground had to be stamped down by thousands of natives before he could use the runway ; and at Tabora, he only just managed to get his plane off the soft earth with barely sufficient flying speed to stagger into the air.

His report on the route was that the time was ripe for opening an experimental service. In particular he was impressed with the enormous opportunities of the stretch from Cairo to Kisumu, of which he said: 'Here is a country where it would be possible to maintain 100 per cent. efficient regularity, and at the same time do a trip in two days that by the present modes of transport takes over three weeks.' This is a stretch of 2113 miles, and is to-day covered by Imperial Airways in exactly two days, so that Sir Alan Cobham's prediction has come true. My own forecast is that, in the very near future, it will be covered in the same ten hours as Flying-Officer Clouston took on his record-breaking flight in the Comet with Mrs Kirby-Green. What individuals can do now, the airlines will be doing to-morrow. Such is the history of all the air routes.

Unfortunately, the first attempt to start a passenger service, in 1927, met with failure, machine after machine crashing almost as soon as it set off. During the following two years, however, the Royal Air Force and the South African Air Force came to the rescue. In the ordinary course of their Service routine flying, they made several highly successful flights over the whole route, carried out with the most admirable military precision and thorough-

battle for the record, which has resulted in times being reduced again and again. Lieut.-Commander Glen Kidston and Lieutenant Cathcart Jones made the then amazing time of 6 days 10 hours in March 1931; Gordon Store, with Peggy Salaman, cut this to 5 days 6 hours 40 minutes in October 1931, after a hair-raising adventure in the bush, where they made a forced landing and had to spend the night; James A. Mollison, via the west-coast route, and my own flight via the west coast, brought down the record to 4 days 17 hours 50 minutes, but as this survey is of the east coast I will not enter into details of these flights here. The west-coast route attracted long-distance record-breaking flights only because of its saving of some six hundred miles.

During the last few years the England–Cape Town record has been broken so often that one almost forgets each individual effort. Such famous fliers as Tommy Rose, Flying-Officer David Llewellyn, Charles Scott, Tom Campbell Black, Flying-Officer Clouston, and Alex. Henshaw have all played their part. Tommy Rose and I had a battle royal for the Cape record, he taking it from me in 1936 when he beat my outward record (of 4 days 6 hours 54 minutes, which had stood since 1932) by 13 hours 16 minutes, and I stealing it again from him in May 1936, by a flight of 78 hours 28 minutes. However, as I flew via the west coast, whilst he took the longer east-coast route, I cannot really claim to have done much better than he did. Tommy Rose is one of the most genial pilots ever known in aviation history and is universally liked. His sense of humour is a byword—one of his best-known 'cracks' was his telegram announcing a delay *en route*: 'Sorry cannot make it, chain come off bicycle.' On my last flight from the Cape I borrowed a chart of his of the Mediterranean which I picked up in Cairo. When I told him of this on my return and thanked him for the loan, he remarked: 'Hope you did not try to keep on the line I drew. I never could draw a straight line!'

Charles Scott and Tom Campbell Black set off in 1935 in their D.H. Comet aeroplane to try to beat all existing times by some amazing margin, but they had bad luck and had to 'jump for it' in the heart of Africa, leaving the Comet to its fate. Later, in 1936, Scott, with Giles Guthrie, took part in the Schlesinger Air Race from Portsmouth to Johannesburg, winning the race in the remarkable time of 2 days 4 hours 57 minutes.

Till a short time ago the holders of the record were Flying-Officer A. E. Clouston and Mrs Betty Kirby-Green (as she then was; she has since married again). In a four-year-old aeroplane they smashed outward, return, and round-trip records, taking 5 days 17 hours 28 minutes for the round flight, flying by the east-coast route.

To-day's holder of the England–Cape Town record is Alex. Henshaw, who, however, flew by the west-coast route.

Let me fly you over this route in your own comfortable arm-chair. Shut your eyes and pretend you are starting with me on a flight from Cape Town to Croydon. It is 10.30 on Sunday night, 10th May 1936. The beautiful and most efficiently equipped airport at Cape Town is thronged with people come to watch our take-off for England. The tiny plane is the centre of a blaze of lights. Red boundary lamps twinkle along the runways, which radiate from the circle at the centre like the spokes of a wheel. As a Cape Town newspaper described the scene: 'Something more thrilling, more dramatic than any situation yet engineered by film producers was provided by Amy Johnson's take-off for the North on Sunday night. The solitary plane, the hangar with its powerful searchlight throwing a revolving ribbon of electricity, the arch of black night, and the expanse of black veld and the silent crowd.' An aerodrome at night has always seemed to me one of the most romantic and dramatic sights in the world, and Cape Town has one of the most beautiful I have ever seen. There is an aura of fascinating mystery in the African sky around, beckoning you to adventures undreamt-of. Taking off in the beams of the dazzling searchlight, we head north for ‘ Darkest Africa.’

Johannesburg is our first stop. How amused its sophisticated inhabitants would be if they knew I had included them in ‘ Darkest Africa ’—no matter how whimsical I made the reference. Johannesburg is an incredible city, a sort of miniature New York, built on its 6000-feet-high plateau. Unfortunately, we see nothing of it except thousands of winking lights, as we land there at four in the morning on Monday. We have flown over the Hex-River Mountains and rolling veld in almost perfect weather, with the revolving beacon at Kimberley airport pointing the way, visible from 130 miles away. The airport at Johannesburg is enormous, so huge that our take-off with full load is not the hair-raising business it might have been at a height of 6000 feet, where the air is more rarefied than at sea-level, so that the propeller does not ‘ bite ’ so well. Our stay at the airport has been very brief—a mere hour, just to refuel, drink a cup of black coffee, and collect the maps for our flight across Africa.

We are now on our second stage, heading for Salisbury, 625 miles away. It is still dark, and heavy mist obscures the moon. We climb higher and higher as the mist thickens beneath us, until the ground is entirely blotted out. The weather report indicates a south-easterly wind, and I make a slight allowance for this, as it seems that I shall be flying several hours without being able to pick up any landmarks. We have no wireless, a luxury you must often sacrifice in a tiny light aeroplane heavily loaded. After five hours' flying, during which dawn has broken and lit up the unbroken sea of clouds below, I become a little worried, as Salisbury should not be far away. We have seen nothing of the terrain over which we have been flying, but are told later that it is rather lovely, but lonely, veld, with many rivers, ridges of small hills, and plenty of bush.

Eventually, the clouds below—in reality thick mist—break up as the sun climbs higher into the hard blue African sky, and we sight a most picturesque town, on the outskirts of which is an aerodrome. Landing to inquire our whereabouts, we find we have been blown out of our course by a strong west wind and have landed at Umtali, a place I long to revisit, as, since I landed there, I have been sent pictures of its beauties enough to make one want to turn back even though on a record flight. We find we are only a few miles from Salisbury, and in a few moments are there, enjoying the hospitality of famed Rhodesia.

Salisbury to M'pika is over beautiful country, but the weather, as so often in this part of the world, does not do justice to its surroundings. Storms gather, and M'pika, a 'dot with position but no size,' becomes nearly impossible to find, hidden as it is in hundreds of miles of game reserves—jungle-country where wild animals abound. We do not, however, see any, as we are far too much concerned with finding M'pika itself, in the heart of the lion country, before dark. Found at last, the half-dozen people inhabiting the lonely rest-house make us welcome and comfortable, and we spend a few hours of refreshing sleep before leaving next morning just before dawn.

We are now heading for Juba, famous for its stories of lions prowling the main streets at night, but now boasting a first-class modern hotel for the comfort of airline passengers. Our day's non-stop flight consists of threading our way in and out of unpleasant magnetic storms, with giant clouds mocking us as we try to escape their grasping paws, the country below us of such absorbing interest that we are tempted to land to explore. Hundreds of miles of flat rolling plain are set here and there with picturesque native kraals, winding footpaths leading from one to the other. We sight numerous herds of wild animals, which swiftly race away as our noisy engine invades their peace and privacy.

Next we see in the dim distance the 19,710-foot mountain, Kilimanjaro, watch-dog over Nairobi, a city I very much want to visit. But we cannot spare the time on this flight. Reluctantly passing it by, we continue over rich woodlands studded with huge volcanic craters, across the Great Rift Valley, with its millions of teeming game, astride the Equator, over the wide expanse of Lake Victoria, passing by Kisumu, the half-way halting-place of Imperial Airways. Here we hurry through thunder-storms, which seem to haunt the desolate region of jungle and swamps that still separates us from Juba—nowhere to land should our single engine fail and doom us to unpleasantly close contact with the rhinos that roam unmolested below and crocodiles that can be counted by the hundred. Happily, no such fate is ours, and we reach Juba, to enjoy a night's well-earned sleep before facing the next day's journey to Khartoum.

At Juba the precious Nile is sighted, which is to be our guide to Cairo. In spite of having this silver thread to follow, the way is not easy to find, as the river's many deviations from a straight line mean that we cross and recross it often enough to grow confused.

The treacherous Sudd, scene of the forced landing and dramatic rescue of General and Mrs Lewin, has to be crossed, then the grass-lands of the giraffe and the elephant. Flying as low as we dare, we vary the monotony of long hours in the air by trying to spot these animals, but find they are impossible to pick out, camouflaged as they are against their natural backgrounds. Gradually the jungle fades into black cotton soil, a few scrub bushes, and finally pure sand and bare rocks. Then for 2000 miles is arid brown desert, through which meanders the Nile, the heat so terrific that by day travel is very bumpy unless we climb high, and by night the moon is obscured by a thick sand-filled haze.

Khartoum, where we land to refuel in the middle of the day, is blisteringly hot, and we are glad to get into the air again, where we can climb into a reasonably cool climate. This is one of the great advantages of the aeroplane, and I always make the most of it. Khartoum to Cairo is over the same featureless desert country, but as we draw nearer to Cairo we pass scenes of rich cultivation along the lower Nile, and such historical spots as Luxor and the Pyramids. In the Sudan we encounter a fierce sandstorm, but I have learned to fly high over these, and we get past it safely. Cairo is reached after dark, and before the moon has risen, but the aerodrome at Almaza is well flood-lit, and we land there with ease.

Ahead of us are still 2200 miles to reach Croydon, and optimistically I plan to fly these in a day, with one stop at Athens to refuel. Leaving Cairo before dawn, we cross the Mediterranean, bucketing into a 40 m.p.h. head-wind. We are too worried about the lateness of our arrival at Athens to have time to enjoy its almost legendary beauty, and after half an hour spent in refuelling we push on our way. It is literally pushing, against a head-wind that seems to increase in strength with every mile we win from it. Range upon range of mountains we cross, bumping about in a cloud-strewn sky, making a bee-line across Europe in a great effort to reach London that night. At last we have to give up the unequal fight. Masses of cloud smother the crests of the Austrian Alps, stretched across our path and cutting off only too effectively our hopes of home for that day. Deciding it is too dangerous to climb through the clouds and run the risk of meeting some mountain side *en route*, I try to thread my way down valleys, only to find my way blocked by curtains of rain and errant wisps from the main cloud mass. Foiled, we land at Graz and enjoy Austrian hospitality, the warmth of which in no small measure compensates us for our bitter disappointment. The next day we continue our way across the ' high-skyway ' of Europe, too much travelled, photographed, and written about to need describing here, and on to our final landing at Croydon.

CHAPTER IV

ACROSS THE SAHARA TO SOUTH AFRICA

I REMEMBER reading in some magazine, when I was a small child, a series of articles called *Tales of the Dark Continent*. The Dark Continent was Africa, the same Africa which to-day is crossed by aeroplanes in less than two days, and the Tales were of Black Magic, strange superstitions, the evil eye, witch-doctors, taboos, and throbbing drums.

It is almost unbelievable that in so short a space of time as some twenty years progress could have made such immense strides. There still remain in Africa parts where the jungle is impenetrable, the desert impassable, where wild beasts roam at will and primitive natives live close to Nature with customs of a thousand years ago. Perhaps, so far as up with petrol from pumps, the pilot taking a hasty English meal in the aerodrome hotel, on the west coast petrol was poured in from tins and casks, the pilot being dependent for a meal on someone having been thoughtful enough to bring out a little food and drink to the landing field—which did not always happen.

But compare this straight-line route with the much more devious way via Marseilles, Cairo, Khartoum, and Johannesburg, and you will see the appreciable difference in mileage—6300 by the west coast as against nearly 7000 miles via the east. As the most important, and often the only, advantage of an aeroplane is its ability to hop over any kind of terrain, it should theoretically follow a path in the air as straight as a crow flies. Unfortunately, however, some time or other it must come down to

CHAPTER IV

ACROSS THE SAHARA TO SOUTH AFRICA

I REMEMBER reading in some magazine, when I was a small child, a series of articles called *Tales of the Dark Continent.* The Dark Continent was Africa, the same Africa which to-day is crossed by aeroplanes in less than two days, and the Tales were of Black Magic, strange superstitions, the evil eye, witch-doctors, taboos, and throbbing drums.

It is almost unbelievable that in so short a space of time as some twenty years progress could have made such immense strides. There still remain in Africa parts where the jungle is impenetrable, the desert impassable, where wild beasts roam at will and primitive natives live close to Nature with customs of a thousand years ago. Perhaps, so far as mere acreage is concerned, the greater part of Africa still remains uncivilised, with even enormous tracts unexplored, but, owing largely to widespread publicity on recent long-distance flights, the general public is apt to think of Africa in terms that would apply to their own towns, suburbs, or villages.

As regards the east-coast route from England to

South Africa, their mind-pictures may not be so far wrong, although few realise how vast, even on that route, are the areas of jungle and desert which separate tiny dots of civilisation like minute islands sparsely scattered in some immense ocean. The west-coast route to Cape Town is, however, almost wholly uncivilised—or was in the days when I flew there. Hundreds of miles—sometimes even a thousand—separate one habitation from the next. Imagine it ! almost three times the distance from London to Glasgow without so much as a hut !

Why, then, should this wild route attract fliers southward bound to break the England–Cape Town record?

There are two main reasons. One is that the total distance is shorter by over six hundred miles, and the other is that the very fact that it is not the beaten path is an attraction to some pilots, who are lured by pioneering adventures as well as by the thrill of breaking a record. Perhaps I ought to add that sometimes, however much a pilot may want to take this route, he may find it impossible to obtain from the authorities a permit to cross the Sahara Desert.

I am, I think, the only person to have made record flights by both of these routes, and in my opinion the most important difference between the two is the psychological one of knowing that, if lost on the east-coast route, there is every chance of your being found, as airlines, roads, and railways traverse the whole course, whilst on most of the west coast you might as well be crossing an ocean for all the help you would get.

Take a map and join up London to Cape Town and you will soon see why record-seeking pilots preferred this route to the orthodox east-coast route. It is possible this way to fly practically a bee-line course from London to Cape Town. A straight line goes down through France, over the Pyrenees to the south of Spain, across the Mediterranean at its narrowest part, to Oran on the north coast of Africa, over the immensely high barrier of the Atlas Mountains, across a thousand miles of blank, featureless Sahara Desert, through the mountainous Cameroon district with its hundreds of miles of wild, inaccessible jungle, masses of it still unexplored and sheltering we know not what strange sorts of natives and wild beasts, on down by the west coast, almost following the coast-line, until finally we begin to reach some civilisation as we approach Walvis Bay and South Africa.

Till very recently aerodromes were few and far between, and most of these had only the most primitive of ground equipment. Whilst the record-breaking aeroplane on the east-coast route was filling up with petrol from pumps, the pilot taking a hasty English meal in the aerodrome hotel, on the west coast petrol was poured in from tins and casks, the pilot being dependent for a meal on someone having been thoughtful enough to bring out a little food and drink to the landing field—which did not always happen.

But compare this straight-line route with the much more devious way via Marseilles, Cairo, Khartoum, and Johannesburg, and you will see the appreciable difference in mileage—6300 by the west coast as against nearly 7000 miles via the east. As the most important, and often the only, advantage of an aeroplane is its ability to hop over any kind of terrain, it should theoretically follow a path in the air as straight as a crow flies. Unfortunately, however, some time or other it must come down to refuel, and its path in the air must therefore be decided by the location of aerodromes. It is this aerodrome question which makes the west-coast route still difficult, although improvements are constantly being made.

On my last flight to the Cape I planned to go there and back by this route, but found it so impossible to work out a practical schedule that in Cape Town I changed all my plans and devised overnight a return via the east coast. The chief trouble was that landing fields for the latter half of the route were few and far apart, and what there were had for the most part been allowed to fall into a very bad state of repair, so that the task of taking off with the load of fuel required to reach the next far-away ground became an extremely dangerous matter. It was this fact alone that caused me to change my plans.

Until recently, very little was known about this route. Its possibilities were realised by several airway companies, but so were its difficulties. The long and dangerous Sahara crossing deterred all but the very adventurous (dangerous, that is, in the early days when engines were not so reliable and radio and instruments not so efficient). After the Government-backed world's long-distance record attempt in December 1929, in a Fairey monoplane, came to grief in the high Atlas Mountains, both the pilots being killed, this range of mountains came superstitiously to be regarded as an almost impassable barrier.

Lady Bailey flew back from Cape Town to England via the west coast in September to January 1928-29, taking her time over the trip and stopping for a holiday wherever she felt inclined. The record flight of James A. Mollison in March 1932 was the first attempt to use this route as an alternative to the east coast in putting up a London–Cape Town record. He had great difficulty in obtaining maps, as much of the ground was unsurveyed, but he secured his permit to cross the Sahara with comparatively little trouble. Later, Lady Bailey made another flight across the Sahara, and was lost for some considerable time, finally being found by pure chance after being given up. After this, the French Government tightened up the regulations for obtaining permits, and now it is necessary to have a deposit guaranteed before a permit can be obtained.

It was in 1932 that I flew to Cape Town for the first time, choosing this route, and flew back a few weeks later the same way. In 1933 Gayford and Nicoletts captured the world's long-distance record in a monoplane, the same type as that which crashed into the Atlas Mountains four years before. This time the plane stayed the course, landing at Walvis Bay after a world's record non-stop flight of 5341 miles.

Some time after this, Captain Lancaster set out alone to fly to Cape Town, but was never heard of again after crossing the Atlas Mountains. Probably, losing his way in the Sahara and running out of petrol, he died an agonising death of thirst, the fate which haunts every pilot every second of the never-ending hours he spends crossing this arid waste.

To-day Alex. Henshaw is the holder of the record, with the amazing time of 4 days 10¼ hours for the double journey.

How many people think of the Sahara Desert as just a flat stretch of sand like a huge extended seashore? Let me try to draw you a picture of this vast tract of thirsty land of most varied surface and irregular relief, of sand and stones, mountains and dried-up river-beds, on which shines down the pitiless sun, sometimes from hard blue sky, more often dimmed by whirling clouds of sand and dust.

Suppose you are leaving at dawn from Colomb Béchar, the French military aerodrome at the foot of the Atlas Mountains, to fly 1155 miles to Gao on the Niger—from the north to the south of the Sahara.

As dawn breaks you are treated to such a vision of beauty that you find it difficult to concentrate on the prosaic tasks of fuelling your plane and preparing for the take-off. Brilliant stars in black velvet sky have gently faded away, gracefully giving first place to the rising splendour of the sun. Knowing full well our poor eyes could not stand the sudden sight of an African sun in all its glory, it first sends out faint warning rays of pearly grey, shading to lemon, then pale rose and dim gold, growing ever deeper and more intense till suddenly, as though losing patience, it bursts with dazzling radiance on the uncaring world.

Breathing the dry, tonic air, you jump aboard your plane, longing to be away in the light blue sky, already feeling the fascination of the desert.

First you will be flying over the oasis belt. Tiny groups of mud huts shining whitely in the glowing sun nestle amongst clumps of towering green palms. Some of the ground between is stony and rocky, much of it covered with a fine film of sand. South of the oasis of Tarhit, to my mind most beautiful of them all, stretch three hundred miles of golden sand-dunes, wave after enormous wave, as though some god had stretched his arm over a restless sea, petrifying its restlessness into waves of stone.

These sand-dunes are not perpetually shifting, as sometimes people suppose. Only the surface sand is subject to continuous change under the influence of the wind. Their topographic distribution is so permanent that some of the highest of the dunes have their own names, and the popular stories about caravans and armies being engulfed in shifting sands must be regarded as sheer imagination, except perhaps for one or two isolated cases in the Libyan Desert.

From the air the appearance of the dunes is exactly that of a choppy yellow sea, and the monotony of the scene quickly becomes unbearable, added as it is to the perpetual worry of engine failure, a forced landing amongst the yielding hills meaning certain death. Imagine it! Pale blue sky hazy with dust, hot sun making the air incredibly bumpy, in every direction as far as the eye can see an ocean of sand!

Far more beautiful is the Saharan 'Sea of Sand' from the ground. Never shall I forget the day I flew to the oasis of Tarhit whilst my plane was being repaired at Colomb Béchar after the accident I had there on my second Cape flight in 1936, in April. With a party of friends, I landed on the military ground just outside the oasis. Bundling ourselves into an army lorry of the kind which ventures far into the desert to explore and prospect, we traversed a stony road banked with rocky hills on either side, scene of much sharp-shooting from natives during the Tuareg rebellions of only a few years ago.

Suddenly, as we rounded a corner, an unbelievable sight met our eyes. Ahead of us, glimmering in the sunshine, lay the white fort of Tarhit, with its crenellated roof looking exactly like an ornament in white frosted icing on a Christmas cake. Beside it the quaint native village, with narrow tortuous fissures separating its mud huts, sheltered under dark green forests of date-palms. To left and right and beyond stretched row upon row of rich golden sand-dunes. Overhead shone a sun which blazed like molten steel in an incredibly blue sky. The colours were so vivid that we could not see them properly without smoked glasses. The sun-glare faded their natural hues.

Driving into the tiny village, we saw a small boy, utterly regardless of the beauty around him, playing the most cruel game I have ever seen. Scores of pretty little sand lizards were shaken out of tins of red sand, where they apparently were kept imprisoned when not wanted for play, and started off in a race. At first I could not understand why they flopped about so helplessly, until I realised that all their legs were broken, 'so that they could not run away' was the explanation. I was next treated to the sight of a frog being locked up in the back of a toy motor-car, which was then wound up and sent whizzing along the ground. Wretched sand-snakes, half-alive, were taken out of jars and stirred up with sharp-pointed sticks for our delectation. With relief we left the village to climb up a sand-dune, swarms of ragged youngsters coming with us, helping to pull and push us up the steep side. At the top the breeze blew softly on the sand, so that each hill looked as though it had a plume of red smoke.

But to resume our imaginary flight.[1]

[1] Please note I am taking incidents from my own flights of 1932 and 1936. The west-coast route has undergone a vast improvement since those days.

Safely across the sea of sand, you have then to traverse a high plateau of absolutely flat hard earth, the Tanezrouft, in the centre of which is the loneliest landing-ground in the world, Bidon Cinq, which is the French for 'Tin No. 5.' Across the Sahara is a track made by wheels of motor-cars and marked at intervals by large tin casks. This track is the one made by the Trans-Saharan Car Service, which takes passengers across once a week during the Sahara 'season'—October to the end of April. 'Bidon V.' is therefore number five of these tins. There is nothing there whatever except a petrol pump, a beacon for aircraft, and a hut for the Arab keeper. Utterly dependent on the car service for his supplies of food and water and for human companionship, he lives a life hard to beat for loneliness and monotony. Once the man left there went mad, and again, another sold his water supply to some travelling Arabs, himself dying of thirst before the next supply reached him.

The description of Bidon V. in the French Guide-book to the Sahara says: 'The "City of Freedom" of Bidon V. has for a flag a windsock, its wide boulevards are those of boundless space, its main street is bordered with petrol tins, its Square of Silence is ornamented with a petrol pump for motorists, its Grand Hotel was formerly known as a railway carriage, and its most beautiful monument is a petrol pump for aviators.

'Bidon V. is lost in the middle of the Tanezrouft, that terrible Desert of Thirst, more than 500 kilometres without sign of life, human, animal, or vegetable.'

At intervals in this vast plain you suddenly meet ranges of rocky, jagged nountains, in some instances rising to 8000 feet above sea-level. Between the ranges run dried-up river courses, indicating that once upon a time the Sahara was abundantly watered.

Beyond the Tanezrouft Plateau, the rocky ground begins to show some signs of sparse vegetation. Straw-like blades of grass appear, and stunted bushes. Gradually the grass grows closer together and bushes become large enough to shelter groups of camels or horses, and herds of gazelle.

Then, so suddenly that it could easily be missed in the darkening light of rapidly approaching sunset, appears the broad bosom of the Niger, and you will probably shout with joy that one dangerous part of your flight is over. Banks lined with crocodiles, enclosing muddy waters reflecting the crimson glow of a gorgeous sunset, lead us on to Gao, another French military aerodrome, where you land for petrol.

Supposing you decide to carry on to Cape Town, you will probably be surprised to come across another desert farther on upon your route. Hundreds of miles of tropical jungles, with violent storms, thunder, hail, and lightning, however, have to be passed before you come to the largely unexplored Kalahari Desert, which you will have to cross before reaching the comparative safety of South African territory.

As an example of what an equatorial African aerodrome looked like in 1936, let us imagine you are landing somewhere in Equatorial Africa.

Circling what must be the landing ground, as it bears the signs of what was once evidently a white circle, you glide down to land. The landing area seems to be in the form of two runways crossing each other at right angles, the only difference between runways and surrounding grass being that the prepared area is of a lighter colour, probably showing that the grass has been ‘ recently ’ cut. In Africa, however, not only does ‘ recently ’ mean many moons ago, but grass grows at a rate and to a height which would at first delight and then be the despair of an English gardener.

Bringing your machine in to land, you will find yourself sinking down and down into the recently mown grass until when the wheels touch ground you will see the grass closing over your head.

Coming to rest very quickly, as the earth itself is as soft as a new-ploughed field, due to the almost perpetual rains, you wait for some sort of welcome. Nothing happens, and no interest whatever is taken in your landing, although, as you rightly guess, yours is the first plane to have landed there for months.

Sitting quietly in the cockpit and feigning death is the method best calculated to bring out assistance with any degree of haste.

Sooner or later a huge African negro, grotesquely clad in some European's discarded pyjamas, saunters out to see what you want. On his finally understanding that you want petrol, oil, food, drink, and sleep, he wanders away. Ultimately some Europeans will probably arrive to minister to your wants, and, after refuelling with petrol and oil from huge casks, taking a drink of some tepid native liquor and a few minutes' rest, made hell by flies and mosquitoes, you say good-bye to your hosts—who on this coast will never take a penny for all their trouble—and deal with the dangers of the take-off.

With difficulty taxi-ing to the extreme end of the runway, you become bogged and find the plane will not turn round into the wind. Summoning all the help available, at last you half lift, half force the wretched aeroplane to face the direction wanted. By this time the wheels have dug enormous holes for themselves in the soft earth, and your machine has to be lifted bodily out and placed on firmer ground. At last, when you open up the throttle for the actual take-off, with engine roaring full blast, the wheels slowly begin to skid forward. Peering ahead through the high thick grass, you mentally gauge how long it will take to lift the plane off the soggy ground. After sliding along half the runway you decide it is hopeless. You will never get off the ground with your load of petrol. Now, what are you going to do? With a smaller amount of petrol you cannot reach your next stopping-place, and there is nothing suitable in between. Loanda, only 250 miles away, is not much help, as you must get farther than that if you are going to attain that record. Benguela, the next field marked on your map, is, as you know to your cost, having been there before, merely an emergency ground full of holes. With a smile you remember your last landing there, when tall negro soldiers were stationed by each hole and ordered to remain there no matter what happened. They faithfully obeyed instructions, even with an aeroplane roaring down on them at sixty miles an hour, threading its way amongst them, and thus choosing a path without holes too deep to pass over safely.

No, Benguela must be given the miss!

The next one is Mossamedes, in Portuguese West

Africa, where you do not want to land, as your last experience there was not too happy. No proper landing ground exists. You just land anywhere that appeals to you on the sand. If you are lucky you have chosen hard sand, if unlucky you will go over on your nose. Having twice escaped that unhappy fate, going to and coming from the Cape in 1932, you do not want to put it to the test again, but you have no choice. You cannot take off from Pointe Noire with enough petrol to reach Windhoek as planned, so here goes! petrol must be dumped and a landing made at Mossamedes.

Eventually, with the load considerably lightened, you have another try. This time the plane moves forward a little more rapidly, and at last, after an agonising few moments, the tail lifts and speed is gained. The end of the runway is in sight and ahead are grass huts, petrol casks, and trees. Will she do it? It is touch-and-go! Staggering drunkenly, she lifts her wheels off the ground, and you struggle to hold her in the air, dipping a wing to clear a hut, making a crazy flat turn to miss a tree, and now again you are on your way, on your way to Mossamedes, of which your last memory was of a kindly Portuguese admirer who brought out for you masses of flowers, boxes of chocolates, and tins of sweets. Grateful, but unable to carry them in the overloaded, crammed machine, you had to grapple with the problem of how to dispose of them without hurting his feelings. Eventually, you remember, you took them, and you think of the fragrant scent of roses almost burying you in the cockpit, bravely trying to drown the ever-present smell of petrol which had been making you feel so sick.

Mossamedes lives up to its reputation. Again a ticklish landing in the dusk on a stretch of sand, which turned out to be about the worst bit you could have chosen, followed by a hair-raising take-off by the light of bonfires, the cockpit again filled with roses.

This time you have enough petrol to make Windhoek, in South-West Africa, but first you must cross a great upland wilderness to the north-west of the Kalahari Desert. Covering fully 120,000 square miles and resembling the Sahara in many ways, the Kalahari differs from the Sahara in having surface soil mainly of red sand, in places overlaid with limestone and shale. The ground is undulating and looks very much like an ocean, grey and brooding, with a heavy oily swell. Parts of the desert are covered with dense scrub, where wild beasts abound, getting water from tuberous and herbaceous plants.

You are flying over this region by night, with the moon obscured by hurrying drifts of clouds, and you are not particularly enjoying yourself, as ridges of shadowy mountains suddenly jump at you in the dark, forcing you to climb higher and higher.

Dawn shows the way to Windhoek, over five thousand feet above sea-level and buried amongst mountains, making landing difficult.

Your chief memories of this place are of falling asleep signing the log-book in the office, and of stepping out of your plane at the end of the runway before taking off. You are bogged and you jump out to see what can be done. Your sandalled bare feet sink into masses of sharp thorns, and with squeals of pain you jump quickly back into the cock-pit, feet on the cushion before sitting down as is your usual custom. Silly thing to do with thorns in your shoes!

Windhoek is apparently noted for its thorns, and airline machines landing there regularly have to have reinforced tyres which will not burst on take-offs and landings.

After this, Cape Town is easy, as, in spite of weather which makes all other sorts up till now mere child's play, you know that your loneliness is over, that if you 'force-land' someone will quickly come along to help you. What a difference it makes to your mentality! You already feel you are there.

It is unlikely that London to Cape Town via the Sahara and the west coast of Africa will become a regular trunk airway so far as the plans of our English companies are concerned. It is more likely we shall run still more frequent services via Egypt and the east-coast route, whilst in the west of Africa we shall content ourselves with services to connect with the projected British Gambia–South American airway.

The Belgian line, Sabena, however, have immediate plans to extend their existing Belgium–Belgian Congo airway to Cape Town.

Since the days I flew to Cape Town the west-coast route has been considerably improved. In March 1937 the Compagnie Aéromaritime was formed to serve the French Sudan and west coast of Africa. Passengers can fly to Dakar by Air France, where they can now join the Aéromaritime service which flies along the west coast of Africa as far as Pointe Noire, calling *en route* at the Gold and Ivory Coasts. This flight is made in Sikorsky S. 43 Amphibians. Amongst the ports of call are Cotonou, Duala, and Pointe Noire, at all of which I have landed, but in 1936 Cotonou was the only one which could be termed well-equipped. To-day there are at least a dozen airports between Dakar and Pointe Noire with up-to-date equipment.

A subsidiary company of Imperial Airways called Nigeria and Gold Coast Limited run a service from the Egyptian Sudan to Nigeria and the Gold Coast, using De Havilland 86's. Air Afrique, African subsidiary of Air France, serves French West and Equatorial Africa. South African Airways and the Portuguese are at present co-operating to equip the portion of the west coast between Loanda and Cape Town with aerodromes and modern ground equipment. When ready, a service will be started to make a circuit between Johannesburg, Windhoek, Lobito, Loanda, Leopoldville, Albertville, Kisumu, Johannesburg, a route already agreed upon by the various governments concerned.

The last record-breaker to Cape Town who used the west-coast route was Alex. Henshaw. In January 1939 he flew a Percival single-seater Mew Gull racing plane to Cape Town, breaking Flying-Officer Clouston's records for outward, homeward, and round-trip flights. He apparently found very well-equipped aerodromes on his route—fortunately for his fast-landing, fragile-looking plane. His time of 39 hours 23 minutes for the outward and 39 hours 36 minutes for the return flights will take some beating, but as ground facilities improve it will become an easier matter to approach these times, if not indeed to beat them.

Chapter V

LINKING THE NEW WORLD WITH THE OLD

If you study a map of the world you will see a variety of possible 'bridges' across the Atlantic Ocean connecting the vast continents of the Americas with Europe and Africa. In the far north you will note that England can be joined to Canada and North America by a series of short bridges between Scotland and Iceland, Iceland and Greenland, Greenland and Canada by way of Labrador. This northern route offers little in the way of trade and is too long to be considered as a serious competitor to ocean liner traffic. Moreover, the winter climate is too severe for regular flying schedules.

South of this is a 2000-mile bridge from the west coast of Ireland to Newfoundland, by way of which London can be linked with Montreal and New York by the shortest possible route. Further south still is a sort of mid-Atlantic series of bridges between England and the Azores, the Azores and Bermuda and New York. Much further south you will see the narrowest part of the Atlantic between the bulging piece of Africa where Cape Verde stretches out its neck to meet Port Natal in Brazil. This is the shortest route of any across either of the Atlantics.

1. Across the North Atlantic

It was inevitable that the North Atlantic, with its two-thousand-mile waste of water separating the New World from the Old, should hold an irresistible fascination for the long-distance pilot. The appeal was that of 'all or nothing'; success and fame and fortune were certainly his; failure—well, it was a good clean end. Many tried. Many succeeded. Some failed, but their failure was but a challenge to others, and plays its part in the great story of the conquest of the North Atlantic by air.

To-day it is an accepted fact that an air passenger service from London to New York is feasible. It is only a question of a year or two before it will be running regularly. Already several successful survey flights have been made by Britain, America, and Germany, and a mail service is scheduled for the summer of 1939. This astounding step forward in progress has been accomplished in the comparatively short space of twenty-nine years, and takes its place as one of the greatest dramas in history. 1910 was the year in which the Atlantic was first assailed by air, when a small airship tried to span the wide ocean.

It was only in 1903 that the miracle of flight in a heavier-than-air machine was achieved. Sixteen years later an aeroplane succeeded in crossing two thousand miles of water non-stop. *That* is a feat well deserving of all the superlatives the English language can produce, but 'colossal,' 'stupendous,' 'magnificent,' and the like have so lost their meaning to-day that words really fail to do justice to such an achievement as fell to the lot of John Alcock and Arthur Whitten Brown.

There had been many previous attempts to cross the Atlantic by aeroplane, both by direct route from coast to coast and via the Azores, but they were all failures, except the flight of an American flying-boat, commanded by Lieut.-Commander A. C. Read, which crossed in stages from Newfoundland to Plymouth via the Azores and Lisbon, where landings were made to refuel. This actually was the very first crossing by aeroplane, but made in stages. Charles A. Lindbergh's flight was the first solo non-stop crossing west to east; James A. Mollison's flight in a light aeroplane in 1932 the first solo non-stop crossing east to west.

It is not my purpose to recount the many flights over the North Atlantic, wonderful as they are;

volumes would be needed to deal adequately with them. I propose rather to tell of the special problems involved, touching on particular flights by way of illustration, and to give a picture of what is being done to-day to bring about a Europe to North America passenger air service, with perhaps a brief glimpse into the future—and not a very distant future.

Many of you who read these pages will have crossed the North Atlantic by boat. You have probably experienced every extreme of weather, and have, no doubt, often marvelled at what might appear at first sight to be the reckless courage of those who have crossed by air, where there is no retreat, no chance to stop and think, and no escape from whatever the elements have in store for them. To those of you who have not crossed the Atlantic, I am going to give a quick pen-picture of my own flight in 1933, so that you can lean back in your chair and visualise what the North Atlantic really means and appreciate some of the difficulties.

First of all was the choice of machine. One, two, or three engines ? Theoretically, two should be better than one, and three better than two, but are they ? Two engines double the risk of engine failure, three treble it. Two engines mean twice the petrol and oil consumption, and three engines require so much fuel that enormous space is needed to accommodate it. We went carefully into the for's and against's—ways and means. Would two, or even three, engines increase our chances of safety? We found that they would not for the first half of the journey, because we could not carry our great load of fuel on anything less than full engine power. Half-way across, we might be able to stagger along with one engine out of action, but it was doubtful.

Then, too, there was the problem of take-off with the huge weight of petrol necessary for a non-stop crossing of more than two thousand miles, because, although the coast-to-coast distance was under 2000, it was nearer 2500 miles from aerodrome to aerodrome. (To-day, of course, there are excellent bases at Foynes on the west coast of Ireland, and Botwood in Newfoundland, with also a first-class aerodrome at Hattie's Camp, Newfoundland, 2020 miles from Foynes.) Would one, two, or three engines give us the best take-off? It was a problem for mathematicians. Intricate graphs were drawn by experts, whose advice we took purely on paper figures. We decided on a two-engined D.H. Dragon.

Next came the problem of instruments. Should we take one, two, or three sets? If we had two sets, each giving a different reading, which of them was the correct one ? It meant trusting to one set, or taking three. Urged by considerations of space and funds, we decided on one set, compromising by taking one or two different types of instrument.

The plane chosen and equipped with petrol tanks and instruments, next came the question of wireless. Its weight was an important factor. Was it worth while ? Was it worth while, too, to have navigation and landing lights ? Regretfully, we decided that we must travel as light as possible, and everything except stark necessities must be sacrificed.

The flight obviously must be attempted during the summer months, for the weather during the winter was impossible to conquer with existing equipment (this was in 1933). The machine was a special job and took months to construct. At last it was ready, and a take-off was attempted. Paper figures let us down, and the undercarriage refused to stand up to the terrific strain imposed upon it. The plane went back for repairs and for strengthening of the 'under-cart.'

Next came a wait of many weary weeks for suitable weather conditions. Without wireless, we dared not risk leaving unless we knew that conditions were reasonably stable. Moreover, as we were flying east to west, against the prevailing winds, we dared not take off if the winds were stronger than an average of 20 m.p.h. against us, as we should not have had enough petrol to reach the other side.

At last came a report that the winds were light and variable. Low cloud and mist were prevalent, but we were most vitally concerned with the winds. We decided to take off. Would the undercarriage stand up to it this time ? Instead of an aerodrome, we had chosen a beach with a seven-mile run over smooth, hard sand. Immediately overhead the sun shone, but ahead were black clouds and fog sheathing the coast-line of Ireland, which should have been our guide for the beginning of the flight.

After a few minutes of tight-held breath we felt the plane lift. Gingerly turning to seek the coast-line, we ran into swirling clouds of mist, spray, and low cloud. Missing a cliff by inches, we climbed carefully and prayerfully, and at last emerged above the clouds into a new world, a wilderness of blue sky staring at a marble floor. Seemingly suspended between the two, we could only judge speed or forward movement by a glance at our air-speed indicator, which showed a speed of 100 m.p.h.

And so we went on ; hour after hour after monotonous hour. Only the air-speed told us we were moving, and the passage of the sun over our heads that the day was running its natural course. Of the restless waves of the Atlantic far below us we saw nothing. Nothing happened to break the awful monotony. Our imaginations ran riot. Were our instruments lying ? Were we really many hundred miles out to sea ? What was below us ? The urge to go down and see became wellnigh unconquerable, but common sense came to the rescue and saved us this waste of time and fuel.

The sun sank slowly towards the horizon. It disappeared, leaving us more lonely than before as it took from us its cheerful face, yet leaving behind light enough to fade the friendly twinkling stars. For we were now very far north, away north of the shipping route, on the fringe of the summer region of perpetual daylight.

Wisps of cloud materialised in front of us and were cut, like so much paper, by our propellers. As though in defiance, the wisps got together, consolidated, until they formed a large angry mass blocking our way. Plunging into its depths, having no alternative, we steadily climbed, eyes glued to flickering luminous figures on our instrument board —pin-points of light on the accuracy of which our safety depended. Hours and hours passed, with nothing to do but keep the compass on its course and the plane on a level keel. This sounds easy enough, but its very simplicity becomes a danger when your head keeps nodding with weariness and utter boredom and your eyes everlastingly try to shut out the confusing rows of figures in front of you, which will insist on getting jumbled together. Tired of trying to sort them out, you relax for a second, then your head drops and you sit up with a jerk. Where are you ? What are you doing here ? Oh yes, of course, you are somewhere in the middle of the North Atlantic, with hungry waves below you like vultures impatiently waiting for the end.

When a petrol tank runs dry and the propeller falters for a moment, you wake up thoroughly, with fear as the alarm-bell. You know you must let the tank run quite dry before switching on to the next, otherwise you cannot be sure of using every drop of precious fuel, for the gauges are not accurate for the last few gallons. Electric fuel gauges accurate to the last drop are amongst luxuries available to-day but denied to record-seeking pilots of earlier times.

At last the long-imagined dawn really came. The sky lightened slowly, very slowly, and revealed a scene of lonely desolation, hard to beat. A ceiling of pale sky dropped down to join a flat white floor, for all the world like a giant's pudding-basin clapped upside down on a layer of dough. Like a fly caught inside, we were trapped within its walls, and there seemed no escape, no beginning and no end. We must have faith in something, so, almost against our will, we followed the compass westwards. Suddenly the floor below us was cut away, and we had a funny feeling we were going over the edge of the world. It was only the rim of the cloud layer—in reality, the famed and dreaded Newfoundland fog-banks, over which we had been flying for many hours—and we could now see, for the first time since leaving the coast, the glint of water thousands of feet below. Straining our eyes, we peered into the dim distance in search of land. We saw peculiar vague outlines which looked like small white islands when the sun touched them, and only as we drew nearer did we realise that they were icebergs. Soon the water was littered with lumps of drift-ice, like a huge bath strewn with soap-flakes.

Flying low down, we had a glorious sensation of speed and movement, now that we had objects to flash past our wings and leave behind. If we had not been so tired, we might have reflected on the peculiarities of speed. What is speed anyway? Only the relationship in terms of movement of one object to another. We were too weary to pursue such a will-o'-the-wisp of thought. It was only important to *feel* we were moving—when you are very tired, it is good to have the senses confirm what the brain already knows. Our brain was telling us, too, that we were very near land, but we needed to see it to be convinced. At last we did. Land was there ahead. Bleak, barren, and inhospitable. A forced landing on its rocks would have been fully as hopeless as one in the waters below, but it was land, and our senses were satisfied. We had crossed the North Atlantic.

Two thousand miles of water at an average cruising speed, against head-winds, of 80 miles an hour. To-day you could cross that ocean in ten hours in four-engined flying-boats. Warmly tucked up in a sleeping-berth, you could go to sleep this side of the Atlantic and open your eyes in the New World—a real new world of which you can be sure, not the ghostly new world which awaited those who failed in the pioneer days.

It has been obvious for years to the main air-line operating companies of the world that rich profits await the first of them to succeed in establishing an air mail, freight, and passenger service between London and New York, or between any of the chief European capitals and the New World. Yet the obstacles have been so great that not even yet have flights gone beyond the record-breaking or survey stage.

1937 saw the beginning of a series of experimental

flights by commercial airlines across the North Atlantic by the direct northern route, whilst a scheduled passenger service between New York and Bermuda, 726 miles, was inaugurated. Pan-American Airways and Imperial Airways worked in close co-operation, on the Bermuda line running the services alternately.

During the summer of 1937 Imperial Airways made ten successful crossings over the North Atlantic with Short Empire flying-boats—the *Caledonia* and the *Cambria*. Pan-American Airways meanwhile made two round trips from New York to Europe by way of Canada and Ireland to England (the same route as Imperials') and one by way of the ' southern arc ' via Bermuda and the Azores, using the famous ' Clipper ' flying-boats which had already proved themselves on the Caribbean and Pacific airways. Pan-American also co-operated with Deutsche Luft Hansa of Germany, who were making a number of survey flights between the Azores and New York, using Diesel-powered seaplanes, the *Nordmeer* and the *Nordwind*. Germany stuck to her method of catapulting her seaplanes, following up successful experiments of this method made in the South Atlantic.

The first regular passenger plane on the Bermuda service left New York on 18th June 1937. The

Bermuda Clipper alternated with Imperial Airways *Cavalier*, both operating the same number of trips per week. The flight is made in five hours, as compared with forty by boat, and the service has become extremely popular, it being to-day no uncommon thing for people to fly to Bermuda for the week-end. Leaving on Thursday or Friday, they can return on Sunday or Monday. It is a surprising but significant fact that the number of passengers returning by air from Bermuda is far greater than the number going there, which seems to point conclusively to the idea that visitors to Bermuda by steamer become so used to seeing the daily arrival and departure of the huge flying-boats, a feature they cannot miss in such a small island, that they become accustomed to the idea of air-travel as the logical way of getting themselves back to the American mainland.

1938 saw further experimental flights, including the historic one of the upper component *Mercury* launched from the lower component *Maya*. The *Mercury* flew from Foynes on the west coast of Ireland to New York in 25 hours 9 minutes, after a brief stop at Montreal.

This flight was important for several reasons. To begin with, it was the first time an aircraft had been launched in such a manner for the crossing of the

North Atlantic. Secondly, it was the first time a commercial load of any appreciable size had been carried (there was a large cargo of newspapers and films). Thirdly, it was the first non-stop flight between Ireland and Canada, and the time of 13 hours 29 minutes from Foynes to Newfoundland was the fastest so far made. The return flight to England was made via the Azores and Lisbon, the whole round trip taking exactly a week and twelve minutes from the time of leaving Foynes.

It is interesting to observe the comments of the various companies on the results of these experimental flights.

Imperial Airways made their flights with such clock-like precision, in spite of their share of bad weather, that a mail and passenger service would seem immediately practicable for at least a summer schedule over the northern route, were it not that there is little room for passengers and mail because of the enormous load of petrol which must be carried for the non-stop crossing. Imperials are, therefore, experimenting with refuelling in the air, which they seem to regard as the solution to the problem.

Pan-American Airways, on the other hand, are striving to cut down fuel consumption by operating at high altitudes, where they will have the advantage of higher speed, smoother air, reduced petrol consumption, and better visibility. The latter is of great importance when it is remembered that a sight of the sky is essential for taking observations of celestial bodies for navigating correctly. Pan-American, in the person of Captain Harold E. Gray, chief pilot of the *Clipper*, decided that, with a choice of two flight levels, say of 5000 feet and 10,000 feet, even though the lower level had the more favourable wind conditions, yet the higher altitude more than compensated for this because of the extra efficiency of the engines and their lower fuel consumption at this height.

Imperial Airways apparently do not agree with this policy if one can judge by the fact that, on one trip in particular where Captain Gray was high above all the bad weather, Captain Wilcockson, chief pilot of the *Caledonia*, stayed below and fought filthy weather for 1500 miles of rain, clouds, and fog. In conformity with this belief that the lower levels are better for the Atlantic crossing, the engines of the *Mercury* were more moderately supercharged before her Atlantic flight in 1938.

Germany's record of experiment in the North Atlantic is a brilliant one. As I have already pointed out, her policy is to use the 'southern route' via the Azores, and utilise catapult ships as air bases, in this way solving the eternal problem of pay-load. In 1928 she sent a Dornier Wal flying-boat to Las Palmas to collect data. In 1929 she inaugurated the system of flying mail ahead of her ocean liners by installing catapult gear on the *Bremen* and *Europa.* The success of the catapult idea led to tests with the S.S. *Westfalen* in the South Atlantic (as related a little further on in this chapter). From 1933 to 1938 the number of crossings made per year by this method rose from ten to one hundred and four.

By 1936 it was felt that the experience thus gained could be put to use in the North Atlantic. Similar catapulting methods were used, and on the 10th September 1936 the first experimental flight was made by the Dornier Do-18 *Zephyr.* Seven other flights were made that year. In 1937 a second series of flights was made, and between August and November of that year fourteen trips were made between Horta and New York. Seaplanes were chosen to give higher speed. In 1938 twenty-eight crossings were made between July and October.

Deutsche Luft Hansa have calculated that, had they been able to take advantage of available payload facilities to carry mail, 2,800,000 letters could have been carried between Germany and North America during these twenty-eight crossings made in 1938.

France has not yet made any commercial crossings of the North Atlantic, although several record-breaking flights have been made from time to time under the supervision of the French Government.

She has, however, gone to the extent of placing a base-ship in mid-Atlantic to collect meteorological data, and is in favour of the ultra-large flying-boat as the solution of the problems of the North Atlantic. The enormous flying-boat *Lieutenant de Vaisseau Paris* was the type chosen to make the first trial flights. France hopes to start an air mail crossing in the summer of 1939.

So far as British airlines are concerned, our main trouble at the moment is that we have not been able to obtain favourable concessions for an Atlantic airline to finish in New York. There is nothing to stop us proceeding with our line to Montreal, as, on this route, we cross only British territory, but passengers for New York would naturally enough prefer to take a line direct to their destination. At the moment of writing, America is offering any other country a reciprocal landing in New York for every crossing she makes to their capitals. Thus, should France, Germany, Holland, and England be interested, as they of course are, America would get four times the amount of traffic allowed to each of her competitors. No agreement has yet been reached, but it is likely that we ourselves will concentrate on our Newfoundland-Canada connections.

Realising that the 'plum' of all airways will more quickly become a profitable commercial proposition to all concerned by a system of co-operation rather than competition, the great airline companies interested have reciprocal agreements, by which each helps the other, with radio, landing facilities, etc., and no one company is allowed to steal a march on the rest by starting a regular service without the agreement of all concerned.

It is only a few short years ago that pilots were called reckless fools to attempt a North Atlantic flight. To-day, it is hardly even an item of news that still another successful crossing has been made. What once was almost a miracle is now a commonplace.

Why has the North Atlantic been so hard to conquer? The reasons are many and varied.

Of major importance, so far as airline operation is concerned, is the question of pay-load. Until recent years it has been found impossible to build a machine which would not only carry petrol enough for 3000 miles non-stop (such a safety margin was deemed necessary in the days before landing grounds or harbours existed on each coastline of the 2000-mile ocean and when meteorological reports were rare and unreliable) but could carry something, over and above fuel, crew, and equipment, which could be sold and so help to make the flight pay. Such we call 'pay-load.' Owing to the improvement in aeroplane and engine design and to the experience gained on countless record-breaking flights, when manufacturers tried ever harder and harder to give longer range to these special machines (there can be no doubt whatever that record flights have 'improved the breed'), at last it has been found possible to build landplanes and flying-boats which are reliable, fast, and can fly 3000 miles non-stop, yet in addition are able to carry some pay-load. We have not yet quite reached the stage where that pay-load is sufficient to make a trans-Atlantic airline pay. The problem of pay-load still remains, and is at the bottom of the endless discussions on the relative merits of landplanes, flying-boats, and airships; on the question of direct non-stop crossings as against refuelling in the air, the use of seadromes, or the Mayo composite aircraft idea. It is also one of the deciding factors in the choice of route.

The ill-fated German airship, the *Hindenburg*, came the nearest to solving this difficulty. If each separate flight could have been dealt with by itself, there is no doubt that profits were made, but the initial cost of construction was so great, and depreciation to be written off so enormous, that all-round figures must have shown a depressing loss. The *Hindenburg* completed ten round trips between Friedrichshafen and Lakehurst in 1936, and had a whole summer's programme planned for the following year. Disaster, however, overtook her at the very outset of the season.

Experience up to the present has shown that land-planes can carry a greater pay-load than can flying-boats, as the whole construction is lighter, but general opinion is that flying-boats are safer for long ocean crossings, and safety is of even greater importance than economy.

Next comes the controversial question of sea-dromes. Let me quote the *Encyclopædia of Aviation* on seadromes: 'Floating airports anchored at sea for the operation of trans-oceanic aeroplane services. Seadromes have been designed for a North Atlantic airway, and are being developed by the U.S. Government.' (This was, however, in 1935, and their construction has not been continued.) 'Their length is about 1500 feet and the width 300 feet. The flight deck is supported on 32 pillars, 103 feet above sea-level, the pillars being telescopic for manœuvring purposes. When the seadrome is in position the pillars are extended by introducing water ballast so that their bases sink 210 feet below the surface. Beneath the unobstructed flight deck there will be hotel accommodation, radio and meteorological stations, hangars and workshops. No matter how rough the sea, the seadromes are so constructed that they remain floating in suspension beneath the surface motion of the waves and have no tendency to roll and pitch, the largest waves passing through the structure unbroken, as they do under the pillars of an ordinary pier.'

Much has been argued about the legal and military aspects of seadromes, or 'floating islands,' as they are often called. According to existing international law, the position is that 'the construction of seadromes may legitimately be undertaken by any state or any private individual, provided always that the latter is under the authority of a state.' Their construction must not interfere with navigation, either maritime or air, but, so far as the North Atlantic is concerned, this would not arise, as the Great Circle course which would be taken by an airline goes well north of the ordinary shipping route. The conditions applied to seadromes, in times both of peace and of war, are exactly the same as those applying to ships, with the exception of any special regulations fixed by international agreement.

For seadromes it can be argued that they solve the problem of pay-load by providing an alighting place for refuelling. Therefore, valuable space is not taken up by unremunerative petrol tanks, but by a paying load of mail, freight, or passengers. Against them are the prohibitive cost, the problem of mooring, the dreary isolation which would be the life of the staff marooned there (a few years ago I saw a film based on this problem; everyone finally went crazy and broke up the whole works!), and the difficulty of protection in time of war.

Now we come to the question of refuelling in the air. For some years Sir Alan Cobham has been carrying out experiments at his aerodrome in the south of England, and claims that he has now surmounted the major difficulties.

As a general rule, an aeroplane can fly with a greater load than it can easily lift off the ground. Therefore, in theory, if a long-distance plane is fuelled from the air, it can carry more pay-load than would be practicable if it had to take off with its full load of fuel in addition. The problem of take-off has always been one of the most difficult Atlantic fliers have had to face. Many have been the accidents on the take-off, and one experienced pilot put the hazards as high as 85 per cent. of the risks of the whole flight. In these days of constant-speed propellers (a similar principle to gear-changing on a car), increased horse-power to lower weight ratio of engines, higher octane fuel, and greater efficiency and reliability of engines and air-frames, the practical problems of take-off with a great load are not so insuperable as they were a few years ago. Moreover, when flying-boats are used, the space available for take-off is almost limitless, unbounded by hedges or trees, but with different risks of varying seas, winds, and tides.

The most recent effort to cope with the problems of pay-load and take-off is the Mayo Composite Aircraft, of which so much has been written in the press that almost everyone must be familiar with the general principle. Severe and strong has been the criticism of this revolutionary idea. Imperial Airways, slated on the one hand for being backward and slow, none the less were equally censured for their vision and courage in ordering a Mayo Composite Aircraft from the makers, Short Bros. Much can be, and has been, said for and against the idea, but it is, at any rate, an effort to solve the question of assisting the take-off of a heavily loaded plane. The actual tests certainly prove beyond all doubt that the idea is practicable, at any rate for the carriage of mails and freight. For the present it would be unwise to attempt the transport of passengers in such a way, owing to the impossibility of landing the machine with a full load should an emergency arise, or even of landing a seaplane in a rough sea were it possible to jettison the fuel without risk of fire. So far as cost is concerned, although the initial expenditure is high, yet it must be remembered that the lower component, which is the flying-boat, is a perfectly normal machine and is capable of carrying on its ordinary work in between launchings. (This is an advantage over the refuelling machine, which is merely a 'tanker.') Secondly, the upper component, the seaplane, need not be equipped with heavy, expensive variable-pitch propellers, as it has no need of them for take-off and climb.

The advantage over refuelling in the air is that it is an easier and simpler matter to separate two already joined components in bad weather or at night than it would be to bring together two separate aeroplanes and then join them, which is what refuelling practically amounts to. In high winds, in fog, or at night, the hazards would seem to be fairly high, and in any weather a great deal depends on the skill of the tanker pilot. However, most of the technical problems have been overcome, and Imperial Airways have decided on this method of fuelling for their North Atlantic service and have already sent tanker machines to their base at Botwood. No passengers will be taken until trials have proved successful.

Let us turn now to that most important question of route. It is well known that the shortest distance between two points on a globe is a great circle. The great circle route from London to New York, unfortunately, takes a line a long way north of the shipping routes, through the fog-banks off Newfoundland, over much barren country and more sea and fog, before it reaches the coast-line of Maine, and thence on southwards to New York. A direct crossing of the North Atlantic is 1980 miles, for which fuel must be carried, together with sufficient margin to reach an aerodrome, and to combat wind and weather.

What are the alternative routes? The direct crossing is by far the shortest. To the north is an alternative route via the North of Scotland, Iceland, Greenland, and Labrador. This route is nearly 1500 miles longer than the direct route. Not only that, but aerodromes and facilities are rare, and the route is impracticable during the winter, owing to the weather and to the fact that part of the route falls within the region of perpetual night. The sole advantage of the route is that most of it is over land, or, at any rate, the stretches of water to be crossed are comparatively narrow. This means that short hops can be made, and the question of taking off heavily-loaded machines does not arise. In addition, a good pay-load can be carried.

Many long-distance pilots have prospected this route, but, curiously enough, it has never had the glamour of the direct crossing. It is not to-day considered a serious alternative to the other two, for the reasons that it is purely a summer proposition; traffic on the way would probably be very small, as so much of the country covered is barren and uninhabited; the difficulties of making aerodromes and harbours and supplying ground equipment and meteorological services are great; the much longer distance to be covered would make the cost of the trip higher and the saving of time over a liner's voyage negligible. After all, time-saving is one thing an airline is expected to offer, and to gain this advantage Atlantic passengers might be willing to pay more and put up with discomfort, but they will certainly not pay more, suffer discomfort, and yet only arrive at the same time as those on a boat—with always the possibility of an emergency delaying them indefinitely!

So much, then, for the northern routes. There remains the southern route via the Azores. Although longer than the direct crossing, it has the great advantage of consistently finer weather, in winter as well as in summer. Moreover, the sea crossing is along shipping routes, where it is easier to obtain reliable meteorological information, and the land route to Lisbon is already well-equipped with aerodromes.

The longest over-water jump in any of the proposed routes is that from Bermuda to the Azores—2106 miles (rhumb-line track distance). The New York–Bermuda section is already in regular operation, and it is very likely that this 'southern arc' will be the future passenger route during the winter.

What of the future? Which route will ultimately be chosen? Will landplanes refuelled from the air, enormous flying-boats like the Dornier Do-X, or seaplanes launched like *Mercury* from *Maia* be the solution to the type of vehicle considered as most suitable, or will airships once more come into vogue? Will airliners supersede ocean liners so far as fast first-class traffic is concerned, or is there room for all? Will the cost to the passenger, the profit to the operator, the incentive to the aircraft and engine manufacturer, ever be great enough to tempt them? And can a high degree of punctuality and safety be consistently maintained winter and summer alike?

All these questions and more are concerning the minds of business men, operators, constructors, and governments in every major country. Amongst the most important of immediate problems are pay-load, take-off with heavy loads, weather conditions (mainly fog and ice), and maintenance of reliable schedules.

To deal with them, experiments are being made with various types of aircraft, as I have already explained; harbours and flying bases have been built and equipped in Ireland and Newfoundland for the direct crossing, and in Lisbon and the Azores for the southern route; meteorological data are being collected and efforts made to give accurate forecasts of weather over the air route (as already shown, this is farther north than the shipping route and therefore ships' data are of little use). Instruments are being improved, in particular wireless and the automatic pilot. De-icing equipment is being perfected, but this still remains one of the most difficult problems to be contended with. Gradually, petrol consumption is being decreased, weight of materials in engine and aircraft construction lowered, and increased efficiency and reliability obtained, which is making it easier to carry an adequate crew and equipment plus some pay-load.

Imperial Airways, working in co-operation with Pan-American, are planning to start an air mail service across the North Atlantic via Montreal to New York in the summer of 1939. Pan-American, with the *Clipper*, have already made some survey flights this spring via the southern route, whilst Imperials are only waiting for the modified Empire flying-boat, the *Cabot*, to complete its tests for fuelling in the air, and for their new fleet of trans-Atlantic flying-boats to be ready, before they too start an experimental air mail service. Experiments have shown that the *Cabot* would take off normally with a total weight of 48,000 lb., and that by fuelling in the air the all-up weight could be increased to 53,000 lb. From this point of view, therefore, this method of fuelling would appear to be justified, but I have pointed out elsewhere some of the difficulties still to be overcome.

A short time ago plans were discussed for making trial Atlantic crossings with the De Havilland Albatross type landplanes, but for the present the idea seems to be lying in abeyance and the flying-boats are to have it all their own way. Three new Short 'G' flying-boats, ordered by Imperial Airways expressly for the North Atlantic passenger service, are rapidly approaching completion. They will have an all-up weight of 71,000 lb., a range of 3200 miles, and a cruising speed of 180 m.p.h. It is an interesting fact that both the base at Botwood and the splendid new aerodrome at Hattie's Camp are entirely free from fog. The famous Newfoundland fog-banks do not extend any distance inland, and advantage was taken of this happy fact when choosing the sites for the new air bases.

Experts' views on the future of North Atlantic air traffic are well summed up by the United States Maritime Commission in their recent almost historic publication, *Aircraft and the Merchant Marine*. So far as competition with ocean-going craft is concerned, they point out that 'Large flying-boats of 100,000 to 250,000 pounds and capable of carrying 40 to 150 passengers may well supersede highly expensive superliners of the *Queen Mary* and *Normandie* class in all cases where speed above that of the cabin class ships is important.'

Thirty years ago the *Mauretania* established the record of 4 days 10¾ hours. The *Normandie* and the *Queen Mary* lowered that record only by some 14 hours. If the horse-power of the *Normandie* were doubled (at a prohibitive cost) the time could only be reduced by 11 hours. As a contrast, flying-boats, even at their present stage, make the trip in 20 hours, and airships have repeatedly crossed in 48 hours. 'Therefore,' say the Commission, 'attention should be given to these ocean air transport questions: The relative reliability, safety, and schedule-keeping ability of aircraft and superliners; the relative comfort of each; the relative cost and pay-load; feasibility of shipping companies adding ocean aircraft to their fleets; foreign landing rights and the place of transoceanic aircraft as an auxiliary to national defense.'

On the subject of safety and reliability, they say: 'With four engines, any two of which can fly the plane, forced landings are most remote, and already the Martin and Sikorsky 'Clippers' in the Pacific have flown 7,000,000 passenger miles without an accident of any kind. The dirigible, of course, cannot make a very satisfactory landing at sea. But the necessity for this is largely overcome by its ability to float in the air with engines stopped. Reliability of aircraft presently available indicates, therefore, that the time is at hand when transoceanic airlines are becoming increasingly practical.'

As concerns comfort, the Report states, after going into the question most thoroughly: 'The comfort to be offered in transoceanic aircraft appears to be equal to that of a Pullman train and, because of the short time taken by a crossing, not inferior to that offered by competing forms of transportation.'

The Report goes into the question of relative cost at great length, and its conclusions cannot be quoted in any short paragraph, owing to the difficulty of finding any true basis of comparison. To attract passenger traffic it is admitted that the fare per passenger must compare favourably with that of an ocean liner, but it must be remembered that the time of crossing is so much faster that here again values are different. In addition, it will be possible to run airliners daily even more punctually than a shipping service.

Apropos of the important question of passenger and mail loads, it is remarked that ' the prediction of volume of this traffic is highly speculative,' mainly because such a vast improvement in transportation between the Old World and the New as is offered by a 24-hour daily service creates an entirely new clientele. Many more people will cross the ocean when they can do so overnight than would otherwise think of doing so. As far as mail is concerned, a one-day service would create a new mail which might even seriously cut into the cable communication services. As for goods, ' little is known of the volume available to aircraft of London and New York newspapers if offered a 24-hour delivery service, or of the volume of style goods, films, news photographs, gold, or perishables ' (and clothes, I should certainly add !).

The conclusion come to by the Commission is so

noteworthy that it ought to be broadcast everywhere in the British Isles to keep us awake. 'It appears that the use of over-ocean aircraft is not only related to shipping in foreign commerce but will be an important part thereof. It is recommended, accordingly, that legislation be enacted to make applicable to ocean-going aircraft the principles . . . of the Merchant Marine Act, 1936. . . . *It is believed that American Vessel owners should not build superliners, but that they might well give attention in the field of high-speed passenger and express transportation to transoceanic aircraft.*'

2. Across the South Atlantic

For several years France and Germany, and now British Airways representing our own interests at long last, have been concentrating on an airway to South America, to take advantage of the rich trade awaiting the first to succeed.

The South Atlantic crossing was generally regarded by record-seeking long-distance pilots as far easier than the North Atlantic. The distance is 1860 miles from coast to coast (Dakar to Natal), as compared with 1980 of the North Atlantic, and, besides the actual ocean crossing being shorter, the total distance from aerodrome to aerodrome was far less. On the South Atlantic the aerodromes lie directly on each coast, so a far shorter total range was necessary. (Until very recently there were no aerodromes or flying-boat bases on the coasts of Ireland and Newfoundland, except for a strip of ground at Harbour Grace, Newfoundland, used by some pilots on trans-Atlantic flights.) Add to this that the prevailing winds blow less strongly and with a reliable constancy and that the major part of the crossing offers sunshine and blue skies, and you can see why this route is easier. Even so, the South Atlantic holds up its sleeve violent electric storms, burning heat, and blinding tropical rains.

The very first crossing of the South Atlantic in a heavier-than-air machine was made by two Portuguese aviators, Commander Saccadura Cabral and Admiral Gago Coutinho, who set out in March 1922 to try to fly from Lisbon to Rio de Janeiro, in four stages, via the Canary Islands, Cape Verde Islands, and St Paul's Rocks. A prize worth about £4000 had been offered by the Portuguese Government for the first Brazilian or Portuguese aviator to fly between the capitals of their respective countries within the period of a week.

They chose a British Fairey C III seaplane, with a Rolls-Royce Eagle engine, but they had bad luck right from the start and finally lost the prize, although they landed safely in Brazil after a most difficult flight lasting two weeks. It is amazing that they could carry out the flight at all in the year 1922, when there were no proper navigating instruments. The Canary Islands and Cape Verde group were probably easy enough to find, but the St Paul's Rocks are just pin-points of land, no larger than a small vessel. Coutinho had invented a special sextant with an artificial horizon, to which he pinned his faith, and they carried out navigation on naval principles. The sextant proved so accurate that it was later used on historic flights of the Dornier Do-X and *Graf Zeppelin.*

In 1926 the Dornier Wal flying-boat made two flights from Spain and Portugal respectively to Brazil, and in 1927 Colonel the Marchese de Pinedo, with two companions, crossed east to west in stages with a Savoia-Marchetti S. 55 flying-boat.

The first non-stop direct crossing east to west was made by the famous French aviators, Dieudonné Costes and Lieutenant Joseph Lebrix, who, on 14th October 1927, flew from St Louis in Senegal, on the west coast of Africa, to Natal in a Bréguet machine, named after Nungesser and Coli, who had perished a little while previously on a North Atlantic attempt.

There followed several more non-stop crossings from east to west—always with the prevailing north-east trade wind—by several French and Italian pilots. So far, no crossing had been made in the opposite direction, no solo crossings had been made, and no British pilot had attempted this flight.

In 1930 the famous French pilot, Jean Mermoz, safely crossed on his first flight for the French Air Company—' Aero Postale ' (later Air France). He made altogether some hundred routine flights before the final tragedy of his disappearance in the South Atlantic put an end to his brilliant record.

In January 1931 bearded General Balbo took his ten Savoia S. 55 seaplanes over in formation, but it was eventually an Englishman, Squadron-Leader Bert Hinkler, who made the first solo flight. Not only was it the first solo flight, and the first crossing of the South Atlantic in an English light plane—he flew a De Havilland Puss Moth with a single Gypsy engine—but it was the first crossing in history from west to east against the trade winds. The first solo crossing from east to west was made in 1933 by James A. Mollison in a similar machine.

Air France machines continued to cross time and again, until the South Atlantic lost any glamour it might ever have had and became just another airline. The Germans, too, began to take a serious interest in this route, and sent out the huge Dornier Do-X again in 1931. The South Atlantic, like the

North, took its toll of lives, but the relentless competition went on. Apart from the few individual flights made to establish records, the story of the South Atlantic conquest from the air is largely the story of French and German commercial enterprise.

The two countries solved the problem of carrying a pay-load in their entirely different ways, each ultimately successful. Each in the first place sent out flying-boats or landplanes, under the command of their ace pilots, to survey the route. Each eventually secured mail contracts, but not even yet are passengers carried by plane on the actual ocean crossing.

France, in the first place, flew mail only overland to Dakar, whence it was despatched by boat to Brazil. By November 1934 seventeen crossings had been safely accomplished by air; in 1935 forty more crossings were made, and in January 1936 the first trans-Atlantic air mail was flown the whole way from France to South America. Jean Mermoz, as the chief pilot of Air France, was mostly responsible for these crossings, and his name will for ever be linked with the first direct air mail crossing of the South Atlantic. The policy of the French company has been to build ever larger flying-boats, capable of making the crossing without refuelling, and in addition, with a pay-load of mails and freight, and eventually of passengers. The hundredth crossing was made on the 20th July 1936, and was the occasion of great celebrations and of the issue of a special air mail stamp, since much besought by philatelists.

Air France can claim the oldest air service in the world, for it was in 1918 that the first beginnings of the South Atlantic air mail service were laid by linking Toulouse to Barcelona. To-day the air mail service goes through once a week in each direction, taking four days from Croydon Aerodrome. Passengers are, as yet, taken only as far as Dakar, and must continue to South America by boat, but it is only a matter of time before they will be flown the whole way. Air France's passenger service is operated in conjunction with the Aéromaritime Company, which follows a route along the West African coast, using twin-engined Sikorsky Amphibians. To Dakar the journey is made in large Dewoitine three-engine liners, cruising at 185 m.p.h.

The story of the German airline, Luft Hansa, is slightly different, although the final results have been the same. They, too, have an air mail service once a week to South America, and they likewise do not yet carry passengers by plane. Passengers were carried for several years on the actual South Atlantic crossing when the *Graf Zeppelin* was in service. After the *Hindenburg's* tragic end, however, the Zeppelin was taken off the line and sent back to her sheds at Friedrichshafen, until helium could be substituted for her inflammable hydrogen.

Whatever may be the general opinion about the use of airships for ocean travel, there is no doubt whatever that they solve many of the difficulties faced by heavier-than-air machines, and, until the *Hindenburg* disaster, Germany's lighter-than-air services across both North and South Atlantics had a record of safety, reliability, and punctuality second to none for any form of transport.

An airship, having more available space than an aeroplane, offers greater comfort to passengers, who are able to walk about, move from room to room, and sleep in comfortable cabins. There is no noise, no vibration to disturb them, and should the weather be very bad or engine trouble occur, the airship can hover motionless until the bad patch is past or engineers have climbed to the engines and rectified the trouble. In addition to this, passengers can take much more luggage, even to large and bulky packages. It was a common practice to transport aeroplanes, motor-cars, and other such cargo on the *Hindenburg* before she met her fateful end. I had myself a passage booked on her for self and an aeroplane for the next voyage out from New York, but my plans were 'of mice and men' and I was fated never to carry them out.

Germany, when she first came into the South Atlantic competition for air traffic, realised that the refuelling problem must be tackled first if heavy loads of mail, passengers and/or cargo were to be carried. Obviously, the whole of the plane's pay-load must not be taken up with petrol and her valuable space with reserve tanks.

She considered the question of seadromes, and eventually hit on a similar but far less expensive method of refuelling. A special ship was sent out and stationed in mid ocean to act as a base for the flying-boat. The plane landed on the sea near the boat, was taken on board, refuelled, and then catapulted off again. The first of these supply boats was an adapted cargo boat, the *Westfalen*, a name which has now become almost as well known as many of the names of flying-boats and aeroplanes themselves.

This service with the *Westfalen* was started in February 1934, and was at first operated fortnightly. Later, a weekly service was established. At the same time, the *Graf Zeppelin* was also making weekly trips with mail, but as she was slower than the flying-boat service, it was decided to use her for passenger-carrying and keep the faster service for mails.

So successful was this refuelling method that another ship, the *Schwabenland*, was fitted out in a similar way. One boat was then stationed just off the African coast and the other off Brazil. The service functioned with such clock-like precision that the same procedure was later adopted for experimental survey flights on the North Atlantic, as already explained.

Just a word here on how this seemingly difficult feat of catapulting off a vessel at sea is performed. The flying-boat or seaplane alights in the wake of the ship on a special 'tow-sail' and is then lifted on board by a crane. It is possible to have three Dornier Wal flying-boats on board at the same time. The engines are inspected and the plane refuelled. It is then placed in position on the catapult runway, ready to leave again. The total length of the runway is 136 feet, of which distance 104 feet form the 'acceleration' runway, which the flying-boat covers in 1.52 seconds. The catapult is worked by compressed air, and can release a machine with a total load of 14,000 kilograms.

The *Graf Zeppelin*, which made its first voyage in 1928, crossed the South Atlantic a hundred and forty times, the North Atlantic seven times, and the Pacific once before being taken out of service. Since then, no passengers have been taken on the South Atlantic service, either by French or German airlines. Germany is suspending her lighter-than-aircraft programme until she can find some substitute for hydrogen, as the United States have forbidden export of their supplies of non-inflammable helium, and no other country in the world has quantities sufficient to fill nearly four million cubic feet of space.

France is busy with a new trans-Atlantic plane designed to carry forty passengers and crew of five, and it would seem fairly certain that the South Atlantic will become a passenger route before the North Atlantic.

Where do we come into the picture ?

Very late in the day we have realised that we are in danger of losing these rich South American markets, the millions of letters transported annually, and future passengers of wealth and importance. British Airways, runner-up of Imperial Airways for concessions of subsidy and mail contracts, are at last busy prospecting the South Atlantic route. With France and Germany for so many years in possession, it is difficult for us to secure the necessary permits and concessions from foreign governments, but we are doing what we can to push through a fast mail service to South America via British Gambia. It still remains to be seen whether we shall succeed in these efforts.

What does it look like, this long air route, the object of longing of three great nations?

Regretfully I have to confess that I have never crossed the South Atlantic, but I know the first part of the overland route, and, for the rest, I will tell you what some famous pilots think about it.

Bert Hinkler, one of the first and most courageous of the pilots in the 'record-breaking era' in aviation history, was the first to attempt the flight in the more difficult direction, *i.e.* against the north-east trade winds. He crossed much territory before ever he came to the shores of the South Atlantic. In his tiny 120 h.p. cabin Puss Moth machine he flew from New York, in October 1931, to Jamaica, 1800 miles. The next stage was 700 miles over the Caribbean Sea to Venezuela. Much of these two hops was flown by night, and he had to make headway through violent rain-squalls. A further 2500 miles took him to Natal, and on 25th November he left Brazil on his lone flight across the South Atlantic. He was twenty-two hours on the way, so had to fly through the night as well as the day. Fierce storms shook his frail wings as a terrier shakes a rat ; mountains of black cloud blocked his path ; jagged shafts of lightning played around him like an expert fencer seeming always about to strike yet withholding the final fatal thrust. With no wireless, or modern blind-flying instruments to help him, it was an amazing feat to reach the African coast a mere ten miles off his course.

A year and a half later, in January 1933, he set off again to fly to Australia. Retiring and modest as usual, he tried to evade press reporters and photographers, and refused to disclose details of his plans. 'Hinkler's hush-hush flight,' it was announced in the columns of the popular press. And hush-hush it was indeed, for Bert Hinkler was never heard of again, until several months later his body and wrecked plane were found on a slope in the Apennines.

Next on the South Atlantic list came Jim Mollison, who described his South American trip as a 'pleasure cruise' as compared with his previous crossing of the North Atlantic in the same aeroplane, *Heart's Content*, a Puss Moth similar to Bert Hinkler's but with larger petrol tanks and therefore longer range. Jim Mollison never lacked the courage to take off on some flight with a heavier load of petrol than anyone had ever dared to take before. He would always say to the plane designers,

'You just put in the petrol I want and I'll get the plane off the ground,' and he always did.

It was in February 1933 that he set off alone from Lympne with Barcelona as his first stop. Past Gibraltar he flew, on through the blazing morning and afternoon, to Villa Cisneros, which he found a most extraordinary place. It was then the prison reserved by Republican Spain for its Royalist and political offenders, but is now a regular Air France halt.

His plan to cross the ocean was to take off at dawn and get as far as possible in daylight, but this was considered inadvisable by Air France officials at the aerodrome, who warned him of the 'Potain noir,' a belt of very unpleasant weather which would have caught him unawares just about nightfall. Following their advice, he left about midnight, and caught torrents of tropical rain the next day, just as had been predicted.

Amelia Earhart crossed the South Atlantic with her navigator, Fred Noonan, on one of the earlier stages of the round-the-world flight on which she eventually disappeared. She flew in the opposite direction, from Natal to St Louis, Senegal, and also paid a tribute to Air France officials by her remark: 'The weather was exactly as predicted by the efficient Air France meteorologist.'

How I wish I could put back the clock and add the South Atlantic crossing to the things I have done. I envy, not clothes, jewels, and luxuries, but experiences lived through, dangers survived, difficulties overcome. Perhaps some day, when the route is opened to passengers—a day not far distant—I may see these smiling South Atlantic skies and these flooding sheets of torrential rain in the safety and comfort of a huge flying-boat, but it can never be the same as a lone flight against the elements, with not only nature, but the whole world against you crying 'Fool!'

CHAPTER VI

THE CONQUEST OF THE PACIFIC

I WONDER if the Wright Brothers, when they lifted their clumsy machine off the ground for the first flight in history in 1903, had even the slightest idea that, in thirty years' time, huge flying-boats would be spanning the vast Pacific. I doubt whether even their fertile imagination and illimitable faith stretched so far.

Even a few short years ago it would have been thought impossible to build a machine, not only capable of crossing such immense distances non-stop, but, in addition, capable of carrying a load of passengers, mails, and freight. To-day we have become so accustomed to the impossible being achieved, and to the incredible becoming true, that we accept as common everyday facts all the wonderful and startling things that science so profusely gives us.

I think it is a pity to lose the romantic side of flying and simply to accept it as a common means of transport, although that end is what we have all ostensibly been striving to attain. In the stirring story of the conquest of the Pacific from the air are all the elements of colour, glamour, and enchantment of the fabled South Seas. Let us forget for a moment that the enchantment to-day is in very truth a fable, and that the traveller to the South Seas of fiction and song will be sadly disillusioned, and try to recreate their spell in the soft blue of Pacific skies. The West has to answer to the charge of vulgarising the East, of shattering its quaint customs and cults, of flood-lighting its shadowy charms and moonlight mysteries. In defence, let us at least plead that, for all we may have taken away, we have revealed something of the heavens, of the changing wonders of the skies.

The Pacific is so vast that, in the words of the famous *International Geography* of H. R. Mill, 'Although the Pacific appears on the map to be thickly sprinkled with islands, these are really grouped along certain lines, with vast vacant breadths of sea between, and it is to be remembered that Magellan, when he left the Strait which bears his name and ventured for the first time on the unknown waters of the Pacific, crossed the whole breadth of the ocean, and in three months of voyaging saw no land except one barren and waterless rock.'

The Pacific, vastly empty as it seems, has a history as old as time. Those thousands of square miles of desert ocean hold secrets at which we can only vaguely guess, of empires lost, of peoples forgotten or never known, of islands and lands now cradled in the mysterious deep.

Clues to these ancient mysteries are to be found in the strange ruins on many of the islands which are left. Hidden in the jungle in the Caroline Islands, for example, are eleven square miles of ruins of what must once have been mighty buildings. On Malden Island, owned by Great Britain, are ruins of temples of a past race. On Easter Island are hundreds of enormous stone images which puzzle all archaeologists, evidence of what must once have been a powerful civilisation. Now the island is barren and incredibly lonely, inhabited by a mere handful of natives who care for a few sheep from Chile, of which country it is a dependency. Wind-swept, remote, and ghostly, it is called 'the mystery island of the Pacific.'

Many scientists have visited Easter Island, but the mystery of these strange carvings remains as deeply hidden as ever. Were it not for the remoteness and inaccessibility of Easter Island, it would rank as one of the wonders of the world.

Easter Island is by no means the only example of ancient glory and culture in Oceania. On many of the other islands are inexplicable intriguing ruins of buildings, statues, temples, roads, and canals. Who built them, and when ? Shall we ever know ? Visited only by the learned and the curious, they have lain for centuries in peace. To-day the flying-machine has stolen their inaccessibility, and who knows whether soon we may not be 'doing' the temples of the Pacific Islands as we 'do' the Pyramids or Niagara Falls ?

The unknown seas have now been charted ; powerful nations have colonised those islands which were found fertile and rich enough to support life and attract trade, and now the wise ones are annexing many a tiny coral isle, hitherto left undisturbed as being too small or too barren to be worth troubling about, but which to-day assume a new importance as possible stepping-stones on the trans-Pacific aerial highways.

Tales of the South Seas, highly coloured by imaginative writers, have given us a romantic and glamorous picture of greenly wooded islets of incredible beauty, where a soft sun always shines in a cloudless blue sky, where warm seas break over coral strands, and sweet music, laughter, and friendliness hold sway. Such tales are not altogether true, unfortunately, and especially since our Western civilisation has largely canned the music, embittered the laughter and turned friendliness to suspicion. Those who fly will be privileged to see the real Pacific, its waters which can be greedy and cruel as well as warm and blue, its skies which can frown and storm as easily as smile, its islands which can starve as well as feed and shelter you, and natives who are just as likely to resist and fight as to cry welcome.

The fascinating story of the conquest of the Pacific by air is largely the story of a few courageous pioneers and of Pan-American Airways.

Imagine, in the year 1928, an Australian pilot twirling round a globe of the world to try to find some place on the earth's surface where an aeroplane had not yet poked in its nose.

In 1928 it was thought that all possible long-distance flights had been made. The North Atlantic had been crossed thirteen times, counting crossings by all routes in plane, flying-boat, or airship; a squadron of three American machines had flown round the world; the North Pole had been surveyed from the air many times—the first time in 1897 in a balloon; the South Atlantic had been flown non-stop from Africa to Brazil; the England–Africa and England–Australia routes had both been flown even in light aeroplanes.

What else was there to do? Where else to go?

Squadron-Leader C. E. Kingsford-Smith and his

friend, Charles Ulm, found their eyes irresistibly drawn to an enormous stretch of blue water covering nearly half the globe—the Pacific, one of the natural barriers deemed impossible of conquest from the air.

The largest division of the hydrosphere, one-and-three-quarter times the size of the Atlantic, the Pacific Ocean measures 9300 miles from north to south—from the Bering Strait to the Antarctic Circle,—and across its greatest breadth, which is at the Equator, it is 10,000 miles. To the north, it is almost landlocked, measuring a bare thirty-six miles across the Bering Strait. This route is the way ' around ' the Pacific.

How could such a vast amount of water be spanned ?

The impossible problem intrigued Charles Ulm, with his great gift for organisation, and fascinated Kingsford-Smith, pilot without peer, to whom the word impossible was merely the spur to achievement.

Naturally enough, they were most interested in linking up their own country, Australia, with the United States. But how to do it ?

Just take a look at the globe. Draw a piece of string across, say, from Brisbane to San Francisco. It crosses approximately 7000 miles of open ocean. Obviously a route had to be chosen where the hops were far shorter than this, otherwise the word impossible, in 1928, would have won. Today, with the world's long-distance record at 7159 miles, it is a different story, but in 1928 it stood only at 3934 miles (Chamberlin and Levine's crossing of the North Atlantic).

The stage of San Francisco to Honolulu, 2408 miles, had already been flown by Lieutenants Maitland and Heggenberger in a Fokker monoplane in June 1927 (the first flight from the American continent to the Hawaiian Islands), and the islands in the Pacific near to the Australian coast had been explored from the air by Group-Captain R. Williams, Chief of the Australian Air Staff, but beyond this, the Pacific was still unknown. There were no meteorological data, except what was generally known from the observations of ships, which is not of a great deal of help to aviators, as it contains no information on such important points as upper air currents and winds, average height and thickness of cloud, or visibility in mists and storms.

'Smithy,' as he was affectionately called by his friends, drew a line from San Francisco to the Hawaiian Islands, from the Hawaiian to the Fijian Islands, and from the Fijian Islands to Brisbane in Australia. A Pacific crossing from Australia to America in three sections could be done, he reckoned.

A machine was needed with preferably more than one engine and with a range of at least 3500 miles to give them an adequate safety margin on the longest and probably most dangerous hop, from Honolulu in Hawaii to Naselai Beach in Fiji, a distance of 3150 statute miles, as calculated by P. G. Taylor, the author of *Pacific Flight* and Smithy's navigator on a later Pacific crossing.

Before the machine could be thought about, however, they needed money, and neither Ulm nor 'Smithy' had any. Having been through the War and afterwards done plenty of odd flying, in the way of a record flight round Australia, wing-walking in California, and airline passenger flying, they each had plenty of experience and skill, but it was not easy, nor has it ever been, to raise hard cash for some 'Big Idea.'

Eventually, after a record flight around Australia in 10 days 5 hours—a remarkable flight in 1927 of some 7500 miles in a patched-up Bristol plane—they were able to persuade the Australian Government to support them. A Sydney newspaper also helped, and no sooner were these promises made than Kingsford-Smith, Charles Ulm, and Keith Anderson set off by boat for the United States to make arrangements for their ambitious flight.

To cut a long story short, a story full of weary

waiting, hard work, and anxiety, it was nine months from the day they landed in California before they were able at last to set off on their great adventure.

These months were filled with efforts to find the right machine for the almost impossible job it would have to perform; then, after they were lucky enough to find Sir Hubert Wilkins willing to sell his three-engined Fokker plane—which had already been used to fly over Arctic Seas and had proved its reliability—they still had to find more money than had already been promised them. This was the most difficult task of all.

For one thing, they were planning the venture at a bad psychological moment. The tragic Dole Race from the American continent to Hawaii had taken toll of seven lives, and public opinion was dead set against any further flights over that fateful ocean. Australia, instead of sending the promised funds, sent urgent appeals to abandon the flight, but Kingsford-Smith had gone too far ahead with his plans to retract. Keith Anderson had already left by boat for Hawaii to report on landing grounds; Sir Hubert Wilkins had ordered a plane for another South Pole Expedition, relying on the payments from the Fokker to pay for the new one, and numerous instruments, radio equipment, maps, charts, etc., had been ordered. They must raise the money somehow.

Eventually they decided to try to break the world's existing endurance record of 52 hours in an effort to raise funds. After an extremely dangerous take-off, with the machine so heavily loaded with fuel that she could barely stagger into the air, or stay there even when air-borne at last, they were forced to land fifty hours later, beaten. Kingsford-Smith always thought of those fifty hours as being some of the worst he ever lived through, and probably the most disheartening thing the whole time was the almost certain knowledge that they must fail because the engines were using more petrol than they had calculated.

They had failed to beat the record and to win the prize-money they so urgently needed, but they had at any rate proved that the *Southern Cross* (as they had named the Fokker—a name destined to become one of the most illustrious in aviation history) could carry enough fuel for the Pacific flight, and that was what they most wanted to know.

Finally the Australian Government sent orders for the plane to be sold. Keith Anderson was recalled home. They were absolutely penniless and had reached rock-bottom.

As sometimes, but oh, so rarely, happens, help came at the blackest moment. They found that a Captain Hancock, a master mariner, wealthy, and interested in the navigational side of the flight, was willing to help them, and they were able to resume their plans. An expert navigator, Captain Harry Lyon, was added to the crew, and also James Warner, an experienced radio officer. All four worked like slaves to get the machine ready, and on the 31st May 1938 they took off from Oakland airport on the first stage of the flight; a simple statement of fact conveying nothing of the work and the heartache which had gone to achieve it. Nor can mere words describe the dangers faced and overcome, the endurance and force of will pressed into being, the heart-beats missed.

The first stage to the Hawaiian Islands was comparatively uneventful, except for the suspense-filled monotony of 27½ hours of flight over a barren waste of water before the 13,825-foot peak of Mauna Kea was sighted and a safe landing made on Wheeler Field, near Honolulu.

The take-off for the next stage was to be from Barking Sands, where there was a longer runway than at Wheeler Field. The machine took off well, but shuddered in some bad bumps a few feet off the sand. Great skill was needed to ease the jolts with the machine in her heavily overloaded condition.

They were now making 'a long shot at a dot on the map' over three thousand miles away, and everything depended on accurate navigation and on the engines keeping up their steady rhythm. The engines, Wright Whirlwinds, were amongst the most reliable engines of that period and apparently gave the least cause for worry to their pilot.

On this stage, the crew had just about everything possible to worry them short of actually coming down in the ocean, and their final safe landing must be attributed almost wholly to the accurate navigation of Lyon, which was carried out in some of the most difficult conditions possible. Not only was the *Southern Cross* mercilessly bumped and beaten by severe tropical storms, lashed by pelting rain, climbing and diving and dodging to the right and to the left in vain efforts to escape the most violent squalls, but there were countless hours when the sky was completely hidden and it was impossible to take any sights so that Lyon could get a definite 'fix.'

Added to all this were two bad scares, when one of the engines spluttered for about eight minutes before resuming its usual steady purr, and a feared petrol leak turned out to be water formed by condensation around the cold petrol pipe. Three hours out from Hawaii the wireless failed, but Warner was fortunately able to mend this. 'Smithy' had certainly picked his crew well. Not one of them failed him, and he was a born leader, always able to get the best and utmost out of his comrades and workers.

A course had been set to pass over the Phoenix Islands, a group of eight islands which they expected to sight about midnight. However, they were never seen at all, and Lyon set a new direct course for Suva, into the computation of which must have gone a large slice of hope, for it had been utterly impossible to keep accurate dead reckoning.

After 32 hours, with only 7 hours' supply of fuel left, the air became warm and heavy, which indicated that the tropic region of Fiji must be near. All looked around anxious for land, and at last a long low smudge was seen on the horizon. Even then it was some time before Suva itself was found, for the Fiji Islands are a large bunch. Then the Albert Park Sports Ground had to be found, an undertaking in itself, but after 34½ hours in the air and a non-stop crossing of the longest stretch of water ever flown, and for the first time in history too, they landed to face the acclamations they so richly deserved.

The take-off on the last stage to Brisbane was from Naselai Beach, 20 miles from Suva. The weather was perfect, the take-off from the stretch of firm hard sand was child's play after so many more difficult ones. Brisbane was only 1700 miles away, which seemed a very short stretch after the one just accomplished, and all were in high spirits as they soared away into the blue Pacific skies, leaving behind their hospitable friends, the white roofs and waving green palms of lovely Fiji.

Alas for so much optimism! It was destined to a very short life. First of all the earth inductor compass failed, making dead reckoning a far more precarious matter, as they then had to rely on their magnetic compasses, which were influenced by metal parts in the cockpit. Instruments in those days were not by any means as accurate as they are to-day, and flying at night or without visibility was in any event a difficult matter.

To make things worse the weather quickly deteriorated, and shortly after nightfall they encountered some of the worst flying conditions they had yet experienced, worse even than on the stage to Fiji. The cool clear sky became cloaked with clouds, the twinkling stars were blotted out one by one, the *Southern Cross* was bumped this way and that by unseen gusts of fierce wind, lifted up, kicked, and dropped again like a football of the gods. So much for the famed blue seas and star-spangled skies of the Pacific!

This weather lasted until dawn, when it improved

slightly, although the sky was sodden and the sea was 'a sheet of lead, grey and forbidding.'

With daylight they all took hope and began to look eagerly for land ahead. Lyon had been unable to take any sights, and when finally they did strike land they found they were 110 miles off their course. However, they were safe. They had flown the Pacific and they had actually reached Australia. Jubilant, they followed the coast to Brisbane, where they landed, almost too deaf and exhausted to hear the cheers of the 300,000 people waiting to welcome them.

Of their plane the *Southern Cross*, which has become one of the most famous aeroplanes in the world owing to the number of wonderful flights she has accomplished, 'Smithy' says: 'She had borne us in safety over 7389 miles of ocean; her three engines had revolved without a fault over 24,000,000 times; she had lifted the heaviest burdens we could place on her; she had flown safely through the fiercest storms and blinding rain; she had answered every call; she had not failed us once and she had herself come through unscathed.'

Kingsford-Smith was later knighted for his work in aviation, but to his friends he was always affectionately known as 'Smithy.' When he went missing on a solo flight to Australia in November

1935, and was finally assumed dead, we all felt we had not only lost the greatest pilot and leader aviation has ever known, but a charming personality which smiled its way through enough troubles and adversities to have embittered any ordinary man.

Before he went on that fateful flight to Australia he was destined to add still more glory to the history of the Air Conquest of the Pacific, and of this I will tell in a moment.

As an entr'acte to Smithy's next flight across the Pacific in 1934 with Captain P. G. Taylor, were several other flights, though none followed the same route to Australia which had been pioneered by Kingsford-Smith and his companions.

In 1929 the airship *Graf Zeppelin* crossed part of the Pacific as a stage in a round-the-world flight. A crossing was made from Los Angeles to Tokyo, the northern route of the Pacific, and with Dr. Hugo Eckener in command, the flight passed almost without incident. So much so, that Major A. E. W. Salt, M.A., noted authority on the world's aerial transport system, said in a book he wrote in 1930: 'Kingsford-Smith and Ulm did what they set out to do, but despite their success, an airship seems to be the natural vessel for such a flight, especially since the *Graf Zeppelin* has flown across the Pacific from Tokyo (Nasumigaura) to Los Angeles, between

August 23rd and 26th, 1929, 5800 miles in 61 hours 57 minutes.'[1]

The *Graf Zeppelin*, advanced product of the advanced mind of Count Zeppelin of wartime fame, made a round-the-world flight in 1929, carrying 20 passengers and a crew of 40 men. Including time spent on the ground, she took 21 days 7 hours 32 minutes for a journey which took Magellan, four centuries earlier, a period of three years.

In 1931 Wiley Post, the almost legendary one-eyed American airman, with Harold Gatty as navigator, flew round the world in a Lockheed monoplane and took the northern Pacific route in their stride, crossing from Khabarovsk in the extreme east of Russia to Solomon Beach in Alaska.

Later in 1931 Hugh Herndon and Clyde Pangborn set out to beat Wiley Post's record. In a Bellanca monoplane they took a terrific chance by flying non-stop directly across the North Pacific, from Tokyo to Wenachee in the United States.

Apropos this flight I could say much, but space and other considerations will not allow. I was in Tokyo when Hugh and Clyde landed there. I had

[1] This distance is considerably greater than the direct great circle route between Japan and North America—5210 statute miles from Yokohama to San Francisco—and this figure must be accounted for by changes of course made by the airship to avoid bad weather.

flown from England across Russia and had been received with garlands of flowers and terrific shouts of 'Banzoi,' the Japanese for 'Hurray.' Almost at the same moment Hugh and Clyde landed at Tokyo's military aerodrome, were seized and put in gaol. Why? Because they had committed the unforgiveable sin of landing in Japan without permission.

This they did because their plans had gone astray, as will happen in the best of well-regulated flights, and they had decided to fly the Pacific from Tokyo instead of going to Kharbarovsk, as previously intended. They barely had the range to do the crossing non-stop, so recklessly decided to 'ditch their undercarriage' to save weight. So long as they crossed the ocean, they cared little if they crashed the other side. That is what I call real spirit!

So soon as they were released, they set off and succeeded in crossing the North Pacific, putting down their plane on the other side, minus its undercarriage, with the minimum of damage. That they had been gaoled by the Japanese seemed a more sensational story than their Pacific crossing, even with its 'do or die' attitude, and they were never, to my mind, given enough credit for their courageous, if reckless, flight.

Following swiftly in their footsteps went Wiley Post again, this time solo, convinced that he could do alone a flight which up till then had needed a crew of trained navigators and wireless experts. He succeeded, but later history has not followed up his claims. To-day, commercial flying relies almost entirely on the navigator and the wireless officer—the pilot is fast becoming little more than ' George ' the robot.

Six United States flying-boats flew non-stop from San Francisco to Honolulu in 1934, under the command of Lieut.-Commander McGinnis. This was one of the first formation flights of an official capacity to indulge in record flying, and as a pioneering venture, can be said to have been efficient, although, naturally enough, it lacked the glamour and romance of a lone effort.

In 1934 ' Smithy ' stepped once more into the Pacific picture. The story of that flight is one of the most illustrious in aviation history. To answer the query of those who are interested in why people do certain things, we would reply that Kingsford-Smith and Taylor made this flight as a protest against red tape, and thereby hangs too long a story to tell in detail here.

Briefly, the *Lady Southern Cross*, successor to the *Southern Cross*, was bought in the specific hope of competing in the England–Australia Race in October 1934. It was necessary for all competing machines to be lined up several days before the start, and the

Lady Southern Cross was late. So late that she was too late, and the reason she was too late was because she was deemed 'un-airworthy' by our Air Ministry, and there were frantic last-minute attempts to comply with the British certificate of air-worthiness requirements. (She was 'un-airworthy' because she did not comply with the loading requirements.)

'Smithy' was never a man to give up an idea once it had bitten into his mind, and he wanted very much to fly his beautiful new aeroplane somewhere. What more natural than across the Pacific, a route he had already explored in a far slower machine, and which he was probably longing to see again—having forgotten all the low-down tricks it had played on him before.

With P. G. Taylor as navigator, and a single-engined Wasp-powered American Lockheed Altair to replace the old *Southern Cross*, Sir Charles Kingsford-Smith once again successfully crossed the Pacific, this time in the opposite direction, from Brisbane to California. It was the second time the Pacific had been spanned between the continents of America and Australia, and both times 'Smithy' was the pilot. To him without any doubt must go the credit for pioneering the Pacific air route to Australia. To-day his dream is coming true, but he is not here to see it materialise. Perhaps it is as well, for credit is rarely given where it belongs.

During his adventurous career he suffered perhaps more than most from jealousy and malice, and it is really only since his death that his true greatness has been appreciated. His friend Charles Ulm eventually perished in the Pacific in 1934, always before him his ideal of the Pacific airway.

The name of yet another great pilot, Amelia Earhart, is written deep in the waters of the Pacific. Not only do they carry the story of some of her greatest flights, but they cherish, too, the secret of her end and enshrine for ever her bright, courageous spirit.

Undaunted by the difficulties related to her by Kingsford-Smith after his dual crossing, she set her heart on being the first woman to fly the Pacific. In January 1935 she flew one stage of it—from Honolulu to California—in her Lockheed Vega, the same machine which had already seen her safely across the North Atlantic in 1932.

Not satisfied with this, she made plans, not only to fly the whole Pacific, but to take it in her stride on a round-the-world flight. In 1937 she laid elaborate plans. A new plane was ordered, a twin-engined Lockheed Electra, and a radio operator, navigator, and second pilot chosen. Her original idea was to fly the Pacific first from Oakland to Honolulu. The next calling point was to be a minute island called Howland Island, half a degree north of the Equator and about 1800 miles south-west of Hawaii. This island is less than a mile by two miles in size, and the chance of finding it after a flight of 1800 miles over open ocean rated her trust in her plane, engines, crew, and equipment idealistically high. The next stage was to be to Australia via New Guinea, and thence on round the world to the west coast of Africa by way of Arabia, across Africa, the South Atlantic, and home via Brazil and the West Indies.

Had she succeeded, the flight would of a surety have been the greatest ever performed, either by man or woman.

The first attempt ended in a failure which would have deterred most from trying again, and Amelia's friends the whole world over, proud as they were that she refused to be beaten, yet shared a secret wish she had not been quite so brave.

The Electra flew the first stage from California to Hawaii, and on the take-off for the second stage to Howland Island disaster overtook them. Whether a tyre blew, or the heavily loaded plane merely swung in a bump on the ground, will never be known, but only a few seconds before it would have been air-borne it suddenly collapsed, and lay broken on the runway. None of the occupants had even a scratch, a testimony to the workmanship of the machine.

With the Electra repaired, Amelia as soon as possible was ready to try again, steadily refusing to see 'the writing on the wall.' This time she decided to reverse the direction of the flight, and to make the Pacific crossing the last stage. The crew was cut down to one navigator, Fred Noonan, and eventually they were off from California across the American continent.

With superb skill she piloted that plane half-way round the world, until again she arrived at the Pacific. The first stage, from Port Darwin in Australia to Lae, New Guinea, was flown in 7 hours 43 minutes, and before them lay 2556 miles to Howland Island, which they were fated never to see. Everyone will remember that futile wait for news, the vain search by American ships, and the final abandonment of hope.

As her friend and fervent admirer, I like to think that her spirit will inhabit those Pacific skies and protect the future Pacific airway.

. . . . . .

Pan-American Airways, America's vast overseas aerial system, has been the one with enough vision to carry out in practice the dreams of these pioneers. Not only are they planning to run an airline to New Zealand over the route pioneered by Kingsford-Smith and his companions, but they have themselves pioneered the route East to West across the Pacific to link up America with her interests in the Philippines and Far East.

First, men were sent out by boat to explore the route, then mechanics were despatched to prepare air bases on the islands selected in mid-Pacific as 'stepping-stones' on the long flight from California to China. Minute coral islands, hitherto of no importance to anyone save myriad flocks of birds and swarms of rats, assumed a new value as vital links in the Pacific airway.

The first stage was naturally from San Francisco to Honolulu, 2408 statute miles.[1] Next came a hop

[1] To those with a passion for accuracy, I should like to explain that figures given for sea-crossings in an Atlas are usually in nautical miles. In planning long-distance flights pilots may work in nautical miles, but more often they keep to the statute mile for the sake of uniformity. Unless the word 'nautical' is specifically mentioned, it is usually taken for granted that the mile is statute. The statute mile is 5280 feet, and the nautical mile is 6080 feet, approximately one-seventh longer than the statute mile.

A second fact to note is that shipping-route distances are calculated from harbour to harbour, whilst air-route distances are reckoned from airport to airport, and the two reports may vary by quite a few miles. For example, Naselai Beach in Fiji, which was used by Kingsford-Smith as a take-off ground on his first Pacific crossing, is twenty miles from Suva. (For most of the figures given for sea-crossings in this book I am indebted to the *Aeroplane*.)

of 1331 miles to Midway Island, so small it is unlisted in *The Pacific Islands Year Book.* The next 1126 miles went to Wake Island, a charming unspoilt island paradise. Actually there are three tiny islands—Wake, Wilkes, and Peale—set within a horseshoe coral reef enclosing the lagoon. The hangar and workshops were erected on Peale Island, also a most luxurious bungalow hotel. Thence followed 1495 miles to Guam. This is a much larger island and has a flourishing export trade in copra, coconut oil, coffee, and sugar cane. It is the largest of the Mariana Group—thirty-two miles long by four to ten miles wide, and is owned by the United States. It is an important naval station and is under the jurisdiction of the Navy Department of the United States.

Manila, in the Philippines, entailed a further stretch of 1600 miles, and eventually the line was extended 690 miles to Hong Kong and inland into China, a total distance of 8650 miles, a third part of the entire circumference of the globe at the Equator.

Harbours were prepared, powerful radio stations built, meteorological data collected, hotels, hangars, and workshops constructed. Huge four-engined flying-boats of the Glen-Martin 'Clipper' type were ordered, and eventually everything was ready for the first experimental flight to be made. In April 1935, Pan-American's star pilot, the late Captain Edwin Musick, left California in a Sikorsky S. 42 flying-boat, and connected up the carefully prepared air bases, until he finally landed at Manila, with the first commercial crossing of the Pacific safely accomplished.

After several experimental flights, mail was carried, and eventually, in October 1936, it was decided the route was safe enough for passengers.

Passengers' reports of their 5½-day nearly 9000-mile flight are illuminating. Never a mention is made of risk, of danger, of unpleasant incident. Spoken of with high praise are the comforts of the 'Clipper' flying-boats, the well-prepared, tasteful meals, the luxury of the hotels *en route*, the beauty and charm of the island bases, the changing wonder of the skies, and, most highly praised of all, the skill of pilot, navigator, and radio officer who, week after week, safely bring home their craft with its precious load. Occasionally, when warning is received of typhoons, the service will be cancelled or a deviation made, but apart from this, the service is run once each way weekly with a most amazing regularity. Navigation is so exact that never once has a 'Clipper' been off its course. The only complaint ever made is of the sheer monotony of the endless hours over changeless seas. In efforts to entertain their passengers, many American air-liners are experimenting with radio programmes, moving pictures, cocktail bars, and organisation of games.

To-day you can leave San Francisco any Wednesday at 3 o'clock in the afternoon, arrive in Honolulu at 9 o'clock the following morning, at Midway Island on the Friday, Wake Island on the Sunday (on this hop you cross the International Date Line and lose a day), Guam on Monday, Manila on Tuesday, and Hong Kong on Wednesday at 3.30 p.m. The present fare is 760 dollars single for the whole journey (*i.e.* about £152), and 1368 dollars return (about £273).

You fly in giant 4-engined, 26-ton, 4000 horse-power 'Clipper' flying-boats. Aboard is a crew of seven; the Captain, whose qualifications exceed those of the master of an ocean liner; under him are a First and Second Officer, a Junior Flight-Officer (a first-officer in training), and a steward. 3800 United States gallons of fuel are carried, enough to leave a reserve of more than 5 hours on the longest hop, and giving a range of 3200 miles. (The United States gallon is five-sixths of the British gallon.) Flying time varies from 18 to 20 hours for the longest lap, depending on the wind.

Waving good-bye to the Golden Gate and great bridges of San Francisco, you climb steadily out to sea, flying high above the deep waters which hide the mysteries of Amelia Earhart ; of Charles Ulm ; of Captain Musick, who disappeared with six of a crew on the *Samoa Clipper* off the Samoan Islands in December 1937 ; of the *Hawaiian Clipper*, commanded by a veteran Pan-American pilot, Captain Leo Terletzky, mysteriously lost in July 1938, between Guam and Manila (this was the first disaster in which passengers' lives were lost since the trans-Pacific service opened in 1936) ; of the United States airship *Macon*, and many others.

Tea, then dinner are served by the steward, and you watch the golden sun drop into darkening blue ocean and see the whole ceiling of heaven light up with millions of dazzling stars. When you are tired your berth is made up for you in your cabin, and, drowsy with the fresh purity of the Pacific air, you sleep till daylight awakens you.

The Hawaii Islands offer you the lovely sight of Mauna Lao, 13,675-foot snow-capped volcano wreathed in clouds, of waving palms, dazzling white beaches drenched in sun-kissed surf. Romantic literature also tells of beauteous maidens who run to greet you with flower wreaths, and sing sweet songs of welcome in your ears. Personally I would sooner shut my eyes and dream of Hawaii than have my enchanting illusions dispelled by a visit.

Beyond the sophistication of Honolulu, you fly into less charted seas. You can see the ocean's floor through crystal-clear waters; have a bird's-eye view of a score of islands, white and green and uninhabited, or hiding some historic settlement or ancient ruin. After lunch you sight Midway Islands—two tiny dots within a circle of white coral.

Here you have time for a swim in the warm, clear water, or a sun-bathe on the soft coral sand. You can play golf, watch the curious gooney birds with which the islands abound, or hunt for souvenirs from some old wreck. Many ships have come to grief on these coral reefs, which know equally well how to hurt as well as to smile. The 'Wandering Minstrel' of Robert Louis Stevenson's *The Wrecker* crashed on these same reefs.

Continuing westwards in the cool of the morrow's dawn, you suddenly lose a whole day without the passing of a second, as you cross the world's half-way meridian of 180 degrees. On and on till the tiny islands of Wake float into view after a 'short' flight of barely eight hours to cover 1185 miles. A mile long, and less than half a mile wide, Peale Isle was unheard of until a few years ago. On the glistening beach you will see beautifully coloured glass balls washed up from Japanese fishing nets. In the transparent water you can glimpse thousands of tropical fish as they flash by, their gorgeous colours scintillating in sun-flecked waves. Here you can bathe, fish, watch the fascinating varieties of birds with which the island abounds (there is a bird sanctuary at the end of the island), ride the 'Wilkes Island Rail Road,' along which all materials for the buildings, supplies of food and equipment were carried, or you can watch life at the bottom of the ocean through a glass-bottomed canoe. Personally, I cannot imagine anything I should like better than a few weeks in this peaceful paradise.

The rugged hills of Guam, which you reach next day after a ten-hour flight, make a contrast to your previous stops. Discovered by Magellan four hundred years ago, it belonged to Spain till after the Spanish-American war, when it became American property. The island is historic and colourful, where water-buffalo-driven carts share the roads with luxurious modern motor-cars.

The approach by air is very beautiful and the island is green and inviting. The 'Clipper' service has been a godsend to its inhabitants, who, though they live more than 5000 miles from the United States mainland, now receive letters in less than a week. Formerly it took a month by an indirect steamer service.

The fifth day brings you to the Philippines, after another ten-hour flight, and here you feel you are really approaching the Far East. There are a hundred islands in the Philippine group, in all of which are sights worth seeing, whilst Manila itself is a most picturesque mixture of early Spanish and modern American.

Five hours more across the China Sea and you are at the gateway to the Far East itself—Hong Kong, junction of the world's airways in the Orient.

. . . . . .

Pan-American's second great trans-Pacific airline, from San Francisco to New Zealand, is in course of preparation. Already several experimental flights have been made, but at the moment of writing no passengers have yet been carried. The project suffered a great blow from the disappearance of the *Samoan Clipper* with Captain Musick, who accomplished so many historic flights, all in the ordinary routine course of his job as chief pilot to Pan-American Airways.

Harold Gatty, navigator to the late Wiley Post on his first round-the-world flight, was sent to New Zealand to conduct negotiations with their Government and to prepare an air base at Auckland. I saw him the last time I was in New York, and shall never forget his saying that he would like the job of cruising all over the Pacific Ocean and planting the American flag on every bit of land he saw, as, sooner or later, it might prove to be of vital importance to some new aerial highway.

On the New Zealand route, the course chosen is from San Francisco to Hololulu, 2408 miles; thence 1056 miles to Kingman Reef—a tiny atoll not even large enough for a land station, and therefore having an auxiliary schooner moored beside it; on to Pago-Pago in the Eastern Samoan Islands, 1558 miles; and then a final 1800 miles to Auckland, New Zealand, a total distance of 6822 miles.

Engineers, radio and weather experts were first of all sent ahead by boat to report on the route, and on the 23rd December 1937, after four years of pioneering work, the *Samoan Clipper* flew out of Honolulu harbour to land in Auckland on Christmas Day.

New flying-boats have been ordered for this route, to carry forty passengers and cargo, and it will certainly not be long before this airline is in operation connecting up the American continent with the British Commonwealth of New Zealand.

Chapter VII

AIRWAYS OF THE BRITISH EMPIRE

The British Isles

In an island 630 miles long by 240 miles wide, which is already a network of good roads and of railway lines operating sixty-mile-an-hour trains travelling by night as well as by day, there is obviously less scope for an airline than over long land or sea stretches or territories where natural obstacles slow down ground transport.

These are the reasons why Britain's internal air traffic has not kept pace with her overseas airlines. However, as aircraft speeds increase and airports become more numerous and nearer to the towns they are meant to serve, our internal services are steadily becoming more frequent, though we are still far from the day when the railways can complain that the air is seriously stealing their traffic.

When you think that Birmingham, for example, is only 113 miles from London and has several fast trains a day making the journey in a couple of hours; that Manchester, 183 miles, is reached in three and a half hours by train, and Newcastle

268 miles, in four hours by 'The Coronation,' and that you can arrive at Glasgow, 401 miles away, in six and a half hours, you can perhaps begin to realise that very little time can actually be saved by travelling by air. Birmingham, theoretically, is only three-quarters of an hour from London in a fast modern aeroplane, but you have to add to this the time taken to and from the aerodrome at either end, and this usually totals up to at least an hour to an hour and a half. It is thus easy to see that no time is really saved over short journeys, and cannot be until there is some more rapid means of transport between airports and city centres. On the other hand, there is certainly scope for 'feeder' services to connect the main cities of the British Isles with Croydon and Heston, whence airlines leave for all parts of the world.

Various suggestions have been made to speed up surface transport between city centres and airports. One suggestion is that special motor roads be reserved for aerodrome traffic, whilst others are in favour of underground railways. One airline company tried out the experiment of an aerodrome alongside the railway line, making special arrangements for the train and air services to co-operate. The two former ideas have proved prohibitively expensive, whilst the latter failed, for one reason because it was not found possible to have non-stop trains to meet every air service, and, for another, because the aerodrome proved to be unsuitable for heavy airline traffic.[1]

Railway Air Services have a service between London and Glasgow via Liverpool of three and a quarter hours from airport to airport. To this must be added the usual time taken to and from the airport, and also we must remember that the total is taken from a business man's day, as the airline does not fly by night. By train, a business man need lose nothing of his working day.

The air services which have always been the most successful in this country are those which offer a really appreciable saving of time over other methods of transport. For example, the most successful route of all is London to Paris, which takes nearly seven hours by train, boat, and train again, as against the latest time of Imperial Airways of seventy minutes between Croydon and Le Bourget taken by the new 'Frobisher' class of airliner, which is replacing the 'Heracles' class.[2]

[1] *I.e.* because the ground chosen for the aerodrome proved to be unsuitable for heavy airline traffic. This experience would seem to indicate that it would be a better policy to bring a special railway line to the aerodrome than try to utilise an already existing railway service.

[2] Air France have just inaugurated a service 'every hour on the hour.'

Another very successful route is the one to Jersey. By air it is a mere one and a half hours, and you arrive fresh and ready for your holiday, or for a week-end away from the strain of city life. The service also brings us out-of-season fruit and flowers at reasonable prices.

Imperial Airways is our main overseas service and is subsidised by the Government. This company does not operate any internal services, but it is responsible for the flying of Railway Air Services aircraft.

At present the Company's Empire services operate from Southampton. There are eight weekly services to Egypt, three to South Africa, and three to East Africa, one to the Gold Coast, five to Palestine and India, three to Burma and Malaya, two to Hong Kong, and three to Australia. In 1939 a regular mail service is being inaugurated across the North Atlantic to Montreal and New York, and, in conjunction with Australian and New Zealand Airlines, across the Tasman Sea to New Zealand. These routes I have described in other chapters of this book.

Imperial Airways started in the summer of 1939 an increased frequency service between London and Paris. There are now eight services in each direction on week-days operated in conjunction with British Airways. These services are operated by the new fleet of four-engined Imperial Airways 'Frobisher' class airliners, which take only seventy minutes for the 205-mile journey between Croydon and Le Bourget, the airport of Paris.

The De Havilland 'Frobisher' class of airliner has accommodation for twenty-two passengers and a crew of four, including a Flight Steward, who serves full-course meals. The four Gipsy-Twelve engines, each of 525 h.p., drive controllable pitch airscrews and give the airliners a maximum speed of 234 miles an hour.

Imperial Airways also operate a daily service in conjunction with Swissair between London and Basle and Zurich, Imperial Airways using Lockheed 14 twin-engined airliners and Swissair using Douglas D.C. 3 airliners. The Imperial Airways services bring Zurich within three and a half flying hours of London.

Le Touquet is connected with London by a summer service operated by Imperial Airways.

Ranking next to Imperial Airways, and rapidly becoming one of the most important international airlines, is British Airways,[1] a recent amalgamation of several lesser airlines, one of which was Hillman

[1] At the moment of writing Imperial Airways and British Airways are in process of being merged into one single corporation.

Airways, on which I myself once flew as pilot for three weeks on the London–Paris airway.

Never shall I forget the late Edward Hillman, the 'bus conductor of the air' as he was often called. A 'rough diamond,' but a most sound business man, he had made a small fortune with his 'bus service,' then, seeing a future in the air, he sold his business and converted everything into an air-line to Paris. Undercutting the fares of all competing companies, he made his own company pay without the help of any subsidy, giving almost a hundred per cent. regularity and safety, although his passengers did not get quite the same degree of comfort as they had on other lines. 'Second-class air travel' he called his service, and an excellent idea it was, too.

Day after day, in all weathers, I turned up in the morning to fly the 9 a.m. service to Paris with full loads of six passengers and baggage in a D.H. twin-engined Dragon plane. I was in sole charge of the aircraft, and used a wireless telephony set to communicate with Croydon and Le Bourget. With no blind-flying instruments such as we know them to-day, and with only telephonic radio communication, no directional wireless, and no blind-landing apparatus, some of those crossings were far more hazardous than my passengers ever guessed. However, two completely reliable engines saved us from trouble.

I was not employed by the company, and gave my services voluntarily because I wanted to keep up my flying and get some more hours in my log-book. After three weeks I felt I had had enough. It is one thing having the responsibility of myself only, and quite another to have to worry about six other people.

To-day, British Airways run very fast services to all the principal capitals of Europe. Operating from Heston Airport, they use luxurious twin-engined Lockheed machines, with the most up-to-date instruments, radio, and equipment it is possible to get. If you ask me why American machines are used for a British service called British Airways, subsidised by the British Government, I should have to reply that we have been so busy building military machines that our commercial markets have been neglected.

British Airways are now moving farther afield with their plans for an airline to Portugal, West Africa, and South America. They also operate the only British night mail service to Berlin and Scandinavia. With Heston as a base, they operate services to Brussels, to Frankfurt and Budapest, to Berlin and Warsaw, to Hamburg, Copenhagen and Stockholm. On the service to Stockholm the saving by air travel is over 33 hours, while on the Budapest service it is 14 hours, and on the Warsaw service 20 hours.

At present the aircraft in service on these routes are Lockheed Electra and Lockheed 14 twin-engined airliners. It was in a Lockheed 14 that Howard Hughes made his record flight round the world.

Now under construction is a fleet of four-engined Fairey F.C. 1 airliners for use on the European routes. These airliners will have accommodation for thirty passengers in a pressure cabin and will be the first British airliners with pressure cabins to go into service. (The reasons for having this particular type of cabin are explained in the concluding chapter of this book.) With four engines, each of 1000 h.p., and a retractable three-wheel undercarriage, the top speed will be 275 miles an hour at 13,000 feet.

A number of the internal airlines in the British Isles are operated by Railway Air Services, a company composed of the four main railway companies, Imperial Airways, and Coast Lines. They run services from London to Glasgow, and also to connect London with Birmingham, Liverpool, the Isle of Man, and Belfast and Manchester.

Isle of Man Services, a company in association with Railway Air Services, operates services linking

Manchester, Liverpool, Blackpool, the Isle of Man, Belfast, Glasgow and Carlisle.

In the south another associated company of Railway Air Services, Great Western and Southern Airlines, runs services linking Birmingham with Gloucester, Cheltenham, Bristol, Southampton, Ryde, Brighton, Bournemouth, Cardiff, Exeter, Plymouth, Land's End, and the Scilly Isles.

Some of these services only operate in the summer months. This is a serious matter for airports which have spent thousands of pounds in equipping themselves for modern airline traffic. Bristol Airport, for example, where I landed at night a short time ago, has complete night-landing equipment, radio communication, customs facilities, and comfortable rest-rooms. Yet, during the whole of the winter months, not an airliner on regular schedule lands there to take advantage of its excellent organisation.

Scottish Airways, with some smaller associated companies, has airlines extending way up to the Orkneys, Shetlands, and the Hebrides. Until a short time ago these seemed as remote to me as they probably do to most of us living in the south of England. Whilst waiting for the start of the Monte Carlo Rally from John o' Groats, I was able to see something of the operation of these airlines, and found that they run with the most amazing regularity in all weathers and are very popular, always being fully booked up well in advance. It is funny to think that in some of these remote parts there are people who are familiar with aeroplanes, but have never seen a train!

Thurso has an airport, as also has Wick, Scotland's 'dry' town, where as usual there is more drinking than anywhere else just because it is difficult to get a drink. I was told that the only difference between Wick and 'wet' towns is, that in the latter you can only get a drink at certain hours, whilst at Wick, there being no hours, you can get a drink any time!

North-Eastern Airways have a service daily from London non-stop to Newcastle, thence to the new Central Scotland airport of Grangemouth to serve Edinburgh, Glasgow, and Stirling, and from there to Perth for Dundee, and finally to Aberdeen. The entire trip, including all stops, takes four hours thirty-five minutes, and is arranged to connect at Perth with the Scottish Airways machine from the Orkneys, and at Croydon with all parts of the Continent.

In addition to these main companies, there are many smaller ones, some operating freight (even racehorses are carried across the Channel), some newspaper services between London and Paris, some taxi and charter services, whilst others offer 'Hire and fly yourself' facilities.

As a general rule, then, we can say that internal airlines in the British Isles flourish at present only where they can offer a faster service than the existing train or boat services, and this only applies over the longer distances, or where natural barriers of mountains, rivers, or seas deprive the railways of their advantage by forcing them into detours, whilst the airline can remain independent of such earthly matters. So far as the future is concerned, it is important to have faster planes and to deal with the problem of more rapid communication between airports and the cities they serve. An immediate need, as already noted, is to provide fast 'extension' services to link up with our Continental and Empire routes. For example, travellers arriving at Croydon or Heston who wish to get to other parts of the British Isles should find connecting services to fly them to their final destination.

AUSTRALIA

Australia, smallest of the five continents, with its satellites, Tasmania to the south, New Zealand to the south-east, and New Guinea to the north-east, has half the world between herself and the

Mother Country. Geography books of the past have remarked of Australia that 'Long ages of seclusion from the rest of the world have impressed on this outlying region a marked singularity in aspect, climate, and natural products. Isolation is the predominant characteristic.'

It is the aeroplane which has brought Australia out of exile. Not only are there to-day fast services linking her with all parts of the world, but her own vast area—2360 miles by 1050—is covered by a most efficient airway system.

It speaks volumes for the development in the aeroplane's performance that Australia has not only become accessible, but vulnerable. Her Government, realising this, is busy building up the Australian Air Force to a high standard of efficiency. Defence estimates, issued in December 1938 for a three-year programme to the end of 1941, announced a total expenditure of £63,000,000, which is a lot of money for a population of seven million people.

Behind Australia's determination to rearm is undoubtedly the fear of Japanese invasion, an ever-present danger of which Australia is far more acutely aware than are we.

Commercial services to Australia are run by Imperial Airways and K.L.M. The portion of the Empire mail service between Singapore and Brisbane is operated by an Australian company, Qantas Empire Airways Ltd.

Imperial Airways have three services weekly from Southampton to Sydney in Empire flying-boats in 9½ days, saving 22½ days on the fastest train and boat service. First-class mails are flown too by these fast services, at the ordinary rate of 1½d. per half oz. The inauguration of the Empire Air Mail scheme was one of the milestones of the year 1938. All first-class mail was to be sent by air without surcharge. When you remember that the previous cost was 1s. 3d. for a half-oz. letter to Australia, you will realise what a revolutionary step forward this was. In 1925 Imperial Airways carried 60,000 lb. of mail. In the year prior to the introduction of the Air Mail scheme, they carried just over a million lb. From figures now being collected since the inauguration of the scheme, it is estimated that this annual figure will rise to 2000 tons. In terms of letters, this means some 180 million letters, each one of which is carried an average of 6500 miles.

In this development, at least, we have led the way, and the increase in air mail carried is justifying the experiment. It is still, however, a controversial matter whether to carry mails separately from passengers. America has usually acted on the opposite principle to ours; she carries the mails separately, with the time-honoured slogan that 'Mails may be lost but never delayed,' whilst passengers may be delayed but never mislaid (the corollary is mine!). Moreover, mails can be carried in sacks and dumped anywhere. Plush-cushioned seats are wasted on them. However, we are going to follow the example of other countries by carrying mails first, so far as experimental services over the North and South Atlantics are concerned.

Holland is setting us a fast pace with their 8-day service from Sydney to London, to be lowered to 3½ days by 1940. Their well-known line, K.L.M., joins hands with Royal Netherlands Indies' Airways (K.N.I.L.M.). They use American Lockheed Electras and giant Douglas D.C. 3 airliners. The fares charged are similar, Imperials being £165 for the single journey (£297, 18s. return), as against £160 charged by Intercontinental Airways, as the combined Dutch lines are called.

I have described elsewhere the actual route to Australia, and here I will try to give you some slight idea of what this vast continent of Australia is like, and what a grand job of work her internal airlines are doing.

A geography book will give us long accounts of her climate, topography, fauna, industries and history, but we are more concerned here with her appearance from the air, her famous pilots, and the uses and scope of her airlines.

The brothers Ross and Keith Smith undoubtedly were the first to make Australia air-conscious by their flight from England in 1919. Sir Keith Smith has survived his brother and is now Armstrong-Vickers' representative in Australia.

Australia has given the world such famous names as Harry Hawker, cheated by fate of his gallant effort to be the first to conquer the North Atlantic; Bert Hinkler, Sir Charles Kingsford-Smith, 'Scotty' Allen, P. G. Taylor, Melrose, who was killed shortly after putting up such an excellent show in the Mildenhall–Melbourne Air Race in 1934; and Edgar Percival, now one of the best-known aeroplane designers in England; and countless others.

A few experimental airlines were run with old war-time planes. Major Norman Brearley started West Australian Airways in 1920, selling out seventeen years later for a vast sum an airline covering 4000 miles, from Perth to Adelaide and Perth to Wyndham. Their fine record boasts of never having killed a single fare-paying passenger.

Queensland and Northern Territory Aerial Services (known as Qantas), from a humble beginning in 1921, has expanded into a powerful company owning to-day seven flying-boats and collaborating with Imperial Airways on the England–Australia airway.

At the time I was in Australia, Colonel Brinsmead was the Controller of Civil Aviation, and a more capable and honest administrator it would have been hard to find. To him personally must go much of the credit for the flourishing state in which Australian aviation finds itself to-day.

Kingsford-Smith, too, did much for aviation, but his airline between Sydney and Brisbane and Sydney and Melbourne (the original Australian National Airways) never outlived the mysterious loss of the *Southern Cloud*, flown by a pilot called Shortridge, with a co-pilot and six passengers, on the route between Sydney and Melbourne, an exceedingly dangerous route in bad weather. The Australian Alps, nearly 7000 feet high and almost always in cloud, separate the two capitals, and with blind-flying instruments and radio services either non-existent or in their infancy, this main-line route proved a most hazardous trip.

Shortridge I shall never forget. His fame as an aerobatic pilot was widespread and I was longing to be 'stunted' by such an expert, so one day I went to Mascot Aerodrome, in Sydney, bright and early in the morning, and let 'Shorty' throw me all round the sky before he left on his ordinary schedule to Melbourne. I never saw him again.

Of the original pilots of this epic airline there remain only a few, amongst them being J. A. Mollison, P. G. Taylor, ' Scotty ' Allen, Lynche-Bloss, and Jerry Pentland—all well known to-day. Kingsford-Smith, Charlie Ulm and Shortridge have spread their wings in another world.

Charles Scott, the well-known long-distance airman, was flying in remote parts of Australia when the great bridge in Sydney harbour was just being built, and when Bradman was ' merely the embryo of the great star he was to become.'

Flying for the Queensland and Northern Territory Aerial Service in 1917, he came to know the northern and central parts of Australia intimately. Travelling out to Queensland by train, he admits to being disillusioned as to the suitability of that country for aeroplanes. ' Everywhere that I could see was scrub and timber, and though the country seemed very flat, there were none of the rolling pasture lands that I had imagined.' But after leaving Charleville aerodrome he says: ' After flying a matter of only thirty miles the timber gave place to the open down country so typical of Western Queensland. Though the country is featureless and uninteresting, it certainly is the paradise of aeroplanes. There are no mountains, and there are blue skies always. The clouds are so rare that they are hailed with thankfulness as a shield from the sun.' Of Queensland he said: 'We had nothing but blue skies and an absolute absence of rain. The whole of the western district of Queensland was suffering from drought. There had been no real rain for three years, and the country which, I was assured, in wet weather was green and beautiful, at this time was brown and devoid of any grass whatsoever. The river beds were dry and the only green visible was the dark green foliage of the coolibah trees on the river banks.'[1]

Having flown from Port Darwin to Brisbane in 1930, I can endorse this picture by Scott. I passed over the same interminable stretches of featureless timber, where a forced landing would have been impossible and a stranded pilot would never have been found. I saw dried-up river beds, and the centre of Australia stretching like a desert forgotten by God and man.

Sir Alan Cobham, on his survey flight to Australia in 1926, found the same difficulty with maps which I had even in 1930. On his return he remarked that a course in path-finding would have been more useful for the back regions of Australia

[1] *Scott's Book.*

than a knowledge of map-reading and navigation. There were no real maps of this part of the world, at least not such as an English surveyor would understand by the term. The maps I was given simply showed a line—my compass course. There were no features to check it by, except, farther south, sometimes a line of telegraph poles or a single-track railway, almost impossible to see in the dense bush. Dried-up river beds were abundant but all looked exactly the same. Towns, marked in important black letters on the map, turned out to be tiny groups of huts. Expecting to find a town of at least 5000 people, you see perhaps three small huts and wonder if you have come to the wrong place.

Longreach, the capital of the sheep district and of Western Queensland, from the air resembles a dump of empty petrol tins flashing in the sun, for all the houses have corrugated iron roofs. There are no trees anywhere and the hot sun beats down mercilessly. In wet weather all roads are impassable.

When I landed at Darwin in 1930 and continued on my way to Brisbane, two of the things that impressed me most were the aborigines and the teddy-bears.

The former I went to see in their compound, where they were doing a war-dance, and it seemed difficult to believe that within the space of a few moments they could doff their warlike paint and wander off to the movies, to amuse themselves with sights far less interesting than they themselves presented.

These dark-brown natives of ancient Australia have long hair, ample beards, and well-shaped limbs. Their affinity with the outside world has always evaded inquiry and their origin still remains obscure. They are fast dying out, but where they have drifted into the towns they are said to make good servants. Many still roam about in their native environment, with their weapons of the Stone Age, and maintain their practice of infanticide and ritual mutilation. They build no homes of any sort, but wander about naked, growing no crops and doing nothing except fashion rough wooden spears, boomerangs, and such tools as they need. They are extraordinarily clever at sending bush messages. How they do this, whether by smoke signals or, as has been suggested, by mental telepathy, is not known.

In some places in the north and centre these bush people are perfectly familiar with the sight of aeroplanes, though they have never seen a motor-car, boat or train, or even a bicycle. I found them a most interesting study and saw quite a few of them. Even as I write this, I have beside me a large frog carved out of wood by an aborigine, and a crude image in their own likeness—souvenirs of a race as old as any we know on this earth, and which is fast disappearing.

As for the koala or tree-bears, these are well known in this country from their pictures. Australia is making an effort to preserve those that remain, and a sanctuary has been built for them near Sydney. They live entirely on the leaf-tips of certain kinds of eucalyptus trees, and there is great difficulty in finding them sufficient to eat. I never saw any real ones, unfortunately, whilst I was in Australia, so, to make up for this, the Australia Cricket Team gave me a stuffed one as a mascot before I left for home, and this I have with me here beside the frog and the tiny model aborigine—not that I need any reminding of hospitable Australia!

Civil aviation in Australia has developed rapidly in recent years, and besides airline operation the aeroplane is extensively used on sheep stations and for medical and ambulance services.

About 50,000 Australians live 'out-back' in isolated settlements, where life was intolerably lonely before the aeroplane and the radio brought the world nearer to them. Sickness and accident had to be treated without medical aid, and gradually a scheme was built up to help these backwoods pioneers. Aeroplanes would fly doctors and supplies out to them or bring patients to the nearest hospital. Each doctor worked an area of 300-mile radius, but many covered far greater distances. Probably most famous among the flying doctors of Australia is Dr Clyde Cornwall Fenton, of Darwin, who pilots and services his own planes and has had many an adventure and saved many a life in the lonely bush.

The centres of population are so far apart that the aeroplane has proved a godsend in the task of making Australia a united whole. It is possible now to make a complete tour by air round Australia, taking less than a fortnight and using only regular airlines.

The chief internal services in Australia are: (*a*) those from Perth, Adelaide, Sydney, and Brisbane respectively, to connect with the overseas services at Darwin; (*b*) the services linking the capital cities of Australia—Brisbane, Sydney, Canberra, Melbourne, Adelaide, and Perth; (*c*) a service from Melbourne to Hobart, the capital of Tasmania.

The most important operating companies in Australia are:

Qantas Empire Airways Ltd., who operate the Sydney–Brisbane–Singapore section of the Empire Air Mail route, and in addition have airlines between Brisbane and Daly Waters and between Cloncurry and Normanton.

Australian National Airways Pty. Ltd. have 'Douglas' services to all the capital cities, and many others besides. This company also operates the service across Bass Strait to Launceston and Hobart. The journey from Melbourne to Launceston takes about a couple of hours by air as against seventeen hours by boat.

Ansett Airways Ltd. have several lines operating from Sydney and from Melbourne.

Guinea Airways Ltd. link Adelaide with Darwin via Alice Springs and the important mining township of Tennant's Creek. This return journey is made in three days, a trip which by surface transport would take weeks.

MacRobertson-Miller Aviation Co. Ltd.'s chief airways are between Perth and Darwin along the west coast, and between Wyndham and Daly Waters.

North Queensland Airways Pty. Ltd. operate several lines from Cairns, and *Airlines of Australia Ltd.* connect Cairns with Sydney.

A new service of considerable importance is the subsidised air mail service from Sydney to New Guinea. Operated by British aircraft, it links up with the Empire service, flying once weekly in each direction. It gives a valuable fast connection between the Mandated Territory, Papua, and Australia.

The total route mileage in Australia for regular airline services is in the proximity of 20,000 miles. Lighting the inter-capital city route is now in hand, and it is anticipated that at no distant date fast night mail services will be introduced.

Flying clubs are the vogue as they are in England, and there are many flourishing airlines carrying mail and passengers between the capital cities of each state, as well as daily services between Melbourne and Sydney and from Port Darwin. Tasmania has an airway to Brisbane flown in daylight hours, a journey of 1400 miles, formerly taking three days by boat and rail. Stores and machinery, animals and furniture are all taken by air to isolated settlements, and one of the most interesting airlines in the world—Guinea Airways—runs services between Adelaide and Sydney, and Adelaide and Darwin, as well as flying tons of mining machinery and equipment into the heart of New Guinea itself. This island, thick with almost impenetrable jungle, was only waiting for air transport to make accessible its rich interior, with its wealth of mineral ore.

The name of Sir Charles Kingsford-Smith, probably the greatest airman who has ever lived, is bound up for ever with Australian aviation. No one did more than he did to set the ball rolling, but he was ahead of his time and did not live to profit by the sound position in which Australian aviation is to-day, and to which he so largely contributed. Such has been the almost overnight growth of aviation in Australia that it is calculated that Australians to-day do more flying per head than the inhabitants of any other country. In 1938, 88,486 passengers flew 8,446,518 miles.

This year will certainly see an airway between Australia and New Zealand, formed by a partnership of Imperial Airways, Qantas, and Union Airways of New Zealand, and before 1940 it is even hoped to extend the service across the Pacific to Vancouver.

Australian aviation is largely controlled by British interests, but fast American transport planes are mostly used and are being ordered in increasing numbers. Sad will it be indeed if we lose entirely this rapidly expanding market, as we still do not provide enough of the type of machine needed—*i.e.* the fast twin-engined monoplane so abundantly produced by America.

New Guinea

The story of the opening up of New Guinea's goldfields by air is one of the most romantic stories in commercial aviation. Mountains, jungle, and hostile cannibal tribes were only some of the obstacles that pilots had to overcome. Mining experts, workmen, mining plant and hydro-electrical equipment as well as stores and material for new townships, and even horses and cattle, were all flown into virgin country and landed on rough clearings made in the jungle.

The first plane to fly from Lae and land at Wau in the goldfields was in 1927, when a D.H. 37 piloted by a war-pilot called Mustar nearly met disaster in landing on the roughly prepared ground. This was the beginning of the development of the goldfields on a large scale. More planes were imported, including many D.H. Moths and a large number of Junkers machines, as it was found that these would carry enormous loads. Traffic increased to 600 tons of goods a month, and the coffers of Guinea Airways began to bulge. In 1935 the approximate mileage flown was 1,303,257 miles.

The use of aircraft enabled the goldfields to be opened up at least a year sooner than would have been possible if a road had been built, modern planes covering the journey from Lae to Wau in twenty minutes.

New Zealand

Considering the isolation of this far-distant Dominion and its difficult physical characteristics, it is remarkable how well advanced in New Zealand is commercial aviation to-day.

For many years it was thought that the mountainous nature of the country, the scarcity of level areas for aerodromes, the turbulent high winds which so often sweep across the mountains, and the smallness of the population, only one and a half million, precluded the possibility of making a success of a commercial airline.

Private flying flourished years before any airline was regularly flown, and commercial flights were usually made by chartering a club or privately owned plane. The Light Aeroplane Club movement, receiving Government assistance for approved clubs from 1928 onwards, played an important part in the development of aviation in New Zealand, not only by providing machines and pilots in the early days and a training school for future commercial pilots, but by giving a much-needed fillip to the civilian population.

The classification of aeroplanes in New Zealand at the beginning of 1938 gives some idea of the proportion of business done by the Light Aeroplane Clubs. Of the machines registered, 43 were owned by clubs, 25 privately owned, 20 listed as commercial planes, and 3 used for experimental purposes.

Such has been the progress in commercial aviation

in the last year or so that these figures now can only be regarded as historical, and have no relation to the fleets of modern airliners to be seen at any of New Zealand's well-equipped airports to-day.

British machines, in particular De Havilland's products, have played the major part in the pioneering of almost every route. Not only is New Zealand very pro-British and anxious to buy at home, but she finds our planes to be specially suitable for conditions in a country where a slow-landing speed and the utmost reliability are essential. Now, such progress has been made in aeronautical science that forced landings rarely happen, and if weather or engine trouble should be experienced, it is nearly always possible to reach one of the chain of landing grounds laid down in 1933 by the Government for their Air Force needs and to aid development of civil aviation.

To-day, De Havilland Rapides and American Lockheeds are mostly used on the airlines, both of which types provide a very high average of efficiency.

New Zealand offers some of the most remarkable panoramas in the world to the aerial visitor. The Wellington–Auckland route, for example, operated by Union Airways Ltd., presents contrasts between rolling plain, fertile farm-lands, and rugged mountain range. Wellington, the Dominion's capital city, enjoys an ideal position as a central airport, since travellers can reach either end of the Islands in a few hours by plane. The aerodrome is at Rongotai, and is amply equipped to deal with the busy traffic of the several airlines using it as a junction as well as a terminal.

Palmerston North, the first stop *en route* for Auckland, has one of the best aerodromes in New Zealand, being situated in level country in rich farm-land territory. Away to the north-west on a clear day can be seen the symmetrical cone of Mount Egmont, rising from the cultivated plain lands below to a height of 8260 feet. This mountain is a well-known landmark to aviators making the Tasman Sea crossing, and must have been hailed with great delight by Sir Charles Kingsford-Smith on his pioneer crossing in 1928.

New Plymouth is the second stop, and also has its aerodrome situated in the midst of level agricultural country. From New Plymouth the route lies mainly over the ocean and along the coast-line with its high cliffs and glimpses of wooded hills towards the interior. Auckland is an important air base and is looking forward to big developments in the future in connection with overseas airlines.

Union Airways also run a service between Palmerston North and Dunedin, calling at Blenheim and Christchurch. The scenery on this route includes the swirling waters of the Sound, separating the North Island from the South ; the plane crosses in thirty minutes. Blue waters glisten against deeply seamed brown mountain ranges, while away in the distance you see the snow-capped peaks of the Kaikouras and the Southern Alps.

East Coast Airways operate between Palmerston North, Napier—the leading seaside resort of New Zealand—and Gisborne, a historic town where Captain Cook landed during his first voyage to New Zealand.

Cook Strait Airways run passenger, mail, and freight services between Wellington, Blenheim, Nelson, and Hokitika along the west coast. This route has some of the most lovely views in New Zealand. Paralleling the whole length of the coast is the Southern Alpine chain, with the mighty 12,369-foot peak of Mount Cook rising in magnificent grandeur above its lesser neighbours.

Along the west coast the aeroplane has done much to bring out-back settlements in touch with the main centres.

In the very near future New Zealand can look forward to the end of an epoch in which she suffered always from a feeling of isolation. Not only is the England–Australia airway to be extended to New Zealand, but she will shortly enjoy a key position in Pan-American's projected Pacific airway from America, of which particulars are given in another chapter.

The stormy Tasman Sea was first crossed in 1928 by Kingsford-Smith, Charles Ulm, and two companions. From that day New Zealand has always kept to the fore in her mind the prospect of a regular mail and passenger service linking up with Australia. In 1938 the Imperial Airways flying-boat *Centaurus* surveyed the route, crossing the twelve hundred miles of Tasman Sea in ten hours. It will not be long now before New Zealand is the terminal of one of our greatest Empire airways, and it is only a question of time before she becomes also an important link in an aerial girdle around the world.

Canada

The development of aviation in Canada has been so different from that in almost all other countries that it is particularly interesting to study.

In Canada the aeroplane has been found more useful for transporting freight than passengers; for surveying and photographing thousands of miles of uncharted territory than for linking up centres of population; for fighting the forest fire, spraying crops with insect-killer, and taking food and medical supplies to lone trappers and traders than for delivering newspapers for breakfast, strawberries out of season, and the latest dress designs from Paris.

The history of aviation in Canada has, until recently, largely been the story of the development of her hundreds of thousands of acres of uncharted territory. Her towns were connected by excellent railway services, their small populations and volume of business making airlines unremunerative.

A population of about eleven millions, spread over an area larger than the United States, which has 126 millions of people, obviously has not the same need for passenger airlines. The above is sufficient to explain why Canada has not until very recently contemplated a trans-continental airline to link up her cities from coast to coast. Other reasons have been the difficulty of making and maintaining airports in areas between the widely spread towns, and the great expense of their construction and equipment.

Canada leads the world in the transport of freight by air. She carries more than any other national air system. The amount of freight and express has grown steadily and rapidly, mounting to over twenty-six million pounds in 1937 from two million pounds in 1931.

The activity in gold-mining particularly has been

one of the chief reasons for this. Another reason is that, whilst normally the carriage of freight is less lucrative than an equal load of passengers, yet in Canada the freight carried is of great intrinsic value, consisting as it mainly does of gold and silver, radium and furs, and such perishables as fish.

Mail, machinery, and supplies are carried into the mining territory and to outposts in the far north, formerly accessible only by canoe in summer and dog-team in winter, involving wearisome journeys of many weeks, and often months. The aeroplane has made a vast difference in the lonely lives of the people of the 'frozen North,' as well as having made it possible to develop and conserve natural resources in parts that would otherwise have been practically inaccessible. It has brought increased business to the trapper, the trader, and the mining prospector; necessities and even luxuries to scattered homesteads; it has aided the sick and, on more than one occasion, has actually saved lives.

These air services of the northern areas had many special features resulting from the carriage of freight as their chief item of cargo. For one thing, the services were a paying proposition, and were unsubsidised. There was, therefore, little Government supervision and practically no ground equipment. Landings would often be made on a lake, or in a clearing, and the pilot would have to pitch camp there for the night, cook, hunt, and fell wood for a fire. Secondly, whilst passengers must be collected punctually, transported carefully to their destination, and landed on schedule, freight needs no such tender care. There was, therefore, little regularity, and when the weather was bad, the pilot would just 'sit down' till it improved and then continue his journey. Any passengers taken on these trips would sit on sacks or packing-cases and be thankful enough to get there in a matter of days instead of months.

Times, however, are changing, and regular services are to-day run on schedule, with all the aids to navigation and safety that modern aeronautical science affords. Passengers too are being considered and given speedy service.

In 1937, Trans-Canada Airlines was formed to operate the long-planned trans-continent air route linking the major cities of the Dominion, from the Atlantic to the Pacific Coast. The line is Government-sponsored and subsidised, and services are to be run daily over a distance of 2688 miles separating Montreal in the east from Vancouver in the west. Mail is already being flown, and the complete line for passengers has just been opened.

The work entailed in preparing ground services

has been costly and laborious. Every hundred miles there is a fully equipped major airport, and at intervals of some thirty-five miles an intermediate landing field. Each of the main airports is equipped with a wireless station, meteorological office, 'teletype' system of broadcasting weather reports, and maintenance and service facilities.

This great airway is of the most vital importance, not only from the point of view of internal communications, which will greatly increase and facilitate trade and business, but the eastern and central portions will be closely linked with the projected North Atlantic airway to Montreal, whilst it is well possible that in a not too distant future Vancouver may be the terminal of a Pacific airway to New Zealand and Australia, thus truly linking our Empire in a chain encircling the globe. In addition to these factors, there is the significant importance of the airway in Canada's and our own defence programmes. Military machines for Britain are being built now in Canada, to be flown across the Atlantic as and when required.

Fast American landplanes have been chosen to operate the service, and even in the winter wheels will be used, as snow can be kept off the runways of the major airports. On the more northern routes skis are used for winter flying, and seaplanes are more common than landplanes owing to the abundance of lakes and rivers and the forested nature of most of the ground. There are approximately 350,000 million acres of forest in Canada, so it can be guessed that aircraft are invaluable for spotting forest fires.

I have done some flying in Canada, but would like to do much more in this Dominion, which attracts me as much as any country in the world. I should like to fly with a ' Mountie,' one of the Canadian Mounted Police, on one of their exciting expeditions, perhaps to spot some smuggler's boat from the air, maybe to trail a poaching trapper, thief, or even a murderer into the wilds. I should like to fly 'way up into the Arctic Circle in the depths of winter, with a load of machinery and supplies which would appal the minds of some of our Air Ministry officials. I should like to meet the ' Bishop of the Arctic '—Dr. A. L. Fleming—who covers his 500,000-mile territory by plane, carrying spiritual aid and, no doubt, material comforts to his scattered flock. I should like to land at some far-distant mining camp with mail, newspapers, fresh cream and eggs for breakfast, and fly on to an Eskimo ' igloo ' in the white wilderness of the far north to collect a £10,000 cargo of luxurious furs. Perhaps, above all, I should like to take out a fast

British plane and attempt some trans-continental records on the brand new trans-Canada airway, for it is a sad but true fact that Canada's airlines are to be equipped with American airliners, and it is high time Britain waved her flag in Canada. With the United States and her machines of advanced design so near, this situation is not surprising, but it behoves us to look well to these markets, not just slipping but rapidly flying out of our reach.

Memories that I already have of Canada are of the excellent airport of Montreal, western terminus of the trans-Atlantic airline and eastern terminus of the trans-Canada line; of flying to Limberlost Camp, landing on a placid lake ringed with cool forest, and enjoying a few days' peace and rest in a log hut, with canoeing, fishing, and riding for recreation. One of the high-lights was meeting Canada's greatest War pilot, Air Vice-Marshal Bishop, V.C., D.S.O. and Bar, M.C., D.F.C., Chevalier of the Legion of Honour, and Croix de Guerre with Palm.

Canada is very proud of her fighting pilots, and she has just cause. Never shall I forget a display of flying at Montreal by three pilots of her Air Force, second to none I have ever seen for skill and precision. The planes they were flying were of obsolete type, but it was easy to imagine what the Canadian Air Force would be like if the steed but matched the rider. This was in 1933, however, and I am informed that to-day no such complaint can be made.

Canada's Air Force is used for a variety of purposes, as well as for national defence. There is a department known as 'Civil Operations,' which covers such varied tasks as patrolling for forest fires, smugglers and poachers in the hunting preserves; 'dusting' crops against insect pests; photographing for maps; mail carrying, experimental flying and exploring, surveying for aerodromes, future air routes, etc. The Royal Canadian Air Force pilot is an all-round man of wide experience, for he uses all types of planes, with wheels, floats, or skis, flies in all weathers, in burning summer heat as well as in ice and biting cold, and can fend for himself—hunt, cook, repair his plane, or render first aid, no matter where he may have to land.

Private flying in Canada developed ahead of airline passenger flying, largely because the Government had the foresight to realise that subsidised flying-clubs and aerodromes would ultimately form the basis for the airlines of the future. In 1927 there were already twenty-three flying-clubs, formed with Government grants and gifts of aeroplanes. Here again most private planes are American.

Aviation in Canada, in spite of the present

defence programme, is essentially a peaceful vision. There are no great fleets of bombers and fighters, few busy airlines carrying queues of business men from city to city, few well-known names of stunt fliers and record-breakers. In Canada every pilot is a pioneer and is breaking records every day without even thinking about it. Every job they do demands courage, initiative, and skill, qualities Canadians have never lacked.

India and Burma

In 1930 I held the record from England to India of 5½ days. You can now fly there in safety and comfort in 2 days 8 hours, a distance of 4780 miles. Even this, however, is not good enough, when you also remember that in 1934 the famous De Havilland Comet aeroplane gave us the record, still standing, of 22 hours.

India's own airways to-day fly from west to east—from Karachi to Calcutta—and from the far north to Ceylon in the far south, with airlines also between Delhi and Bombay, and from Karachi to the Punjab.

Burma also has 'feeder' services from Rangoon and Moulmein to towns up-country.

Indian National Airways was formed in 1933, and Indian personnel is employed as far as possible.

Before 1933, civil aviation in India was a long way behind that of our other Dominions, in spite of the trunk airlines spanning its width *en route* for the Far East and Australia. Even in 1934, when I landed at Allahabad during the England–Australia Air Race and had to retire on account of engine trouble, I was amazed by the Indian attitude to aviation. When we arrived, the aerodrome was gay with the tents and awnings of wealthy maharajahs and princes come to 'watch the race.' Bitterly disappointed at all lack of spectacular skirmishes with death, they soon packed up their tents and faded away (even though Allahabad saw more excitement than any other place, in the burning up of a Dutch plane and our landing with one engine out of action). They left the aerodrome a sad and sorry sight, with vultures hovering in the hard blue sky above a scene reminiscent of some fair ground on the morning after the bright fair has passed on its way.

Even to-day there is no night-flying done in India on any of the routes, owing to lack of night-flying facilities, but development in civil aviation is becoming much more rapid, aided by many of the ruling princes, in particular the Maharajah of Jodhpur, who maintains a fleet of aircraft and has one of the best equipped aerodromes in India.

The growth of private flying and of the flying-club movement in India was encouraged a great deal by Lord and Lady Willingdon. Interest amongst the Indian pilots was stimulated by races and record-flights, for which money prizes were given, whilst every year there is a race for the Viceroy's Challenge Trophy, corresponding to the King's Cup Air Race in Great Britain.

In Burma, seaplanes are found the most suitable type of aircraft, and from Rangoon, Irrawaddy Flotilla and Airways Ltd. operate services.

In the summer of 1934 a remarkable service was operated called Himalaya Airways, its main function being to carry pilgrims from Hardwar to Gauchar, to the sacred places near the source of the River Ganges in the Himalayas. Although the distance was only eighty miles, the trail through difficult mountain passes used to take the pilgrims ten days of hard travel. Whilst the service was being run, other sites for landing grounds were surveyed. In 1935 nearly 3000 pilgrims were carried and 352 hours flown.

Africa

Taking the continent of Africa as a whole, the main trunk routes are those of Imperial Airways to South Africa via Egypt and the east coast, with a branch line striking westwards to the Gold Coast; Sabena's romantic airway across the Sahara to the Belgian Congo; Air France lines to West and Central Africa and south-eastwards to Madagascar; and Italy's new route from Rome to Addis Ababa in Abyssinia.

Besides these main trunk lines, there are thousands of miles of airways operated by the various countries which together comprise the vast continent of Africa.

I have described in other chapters Imperial Airways' great route to Durban. Khartoum, at the merging of the Blue and White Niles, is the air-junction for West Africa. One line continues eastward to the coast, then southward to Durban, whilst the other strikes westward to Fort Lamy and Kano to Lagos, the capital of Nigeria. Thence it extends to Accra on the Gold Coast, and a further extension to Bathurst in British Gambia is probable in the near future in order to connect with the future South Atlantic service to South America.

The second great air-junction on Imperials' trunk route is Kisumu on the shores of Lake Victoria—the second largest fresh-water lake in the world. From this aerodrome you can take a plane of Wilson Airways to Nairobi, capital of Kenya; to the southern shores of Lake Victoria; southward into Northern Rhodesia, or down the coast to Dar-es-Salaam.

Lusaka, the capital of Northern Rhodesia, is the junction in its turn for the line of Rhodesia and Nyasaland Airways to Salisbury in Southern Rhodesia and into Nyasaland. South African Airways also have a route from Kisumu to Livingstone on the Zambesi River, Bulawayo, and Johannesburg.

When I flew back from South Africa in 1936, Imperial Airways had not then inaugurated their flying-boat service, which to-day flies you 7266 miles from Southampton to Durban in five days. The boats deviate from the overland route at Kisumu, flying eastwards to the coast via Nairobi, Mombasa, and southwards following the coast-line to Durban, calling at Mozambique and Lourenço Marques. From Durban you can continue to Cape Town and the principal towns of South Africa by South African Airways.

Air France runs a service to West Africa in connection with her South American airway, the West African terminal being at Dakar in French Senegal. Aéromaritime then fly along the coast as far as Pointe Noire. In association with Air Afrique, Sabena, and Madagascar Air Lines, she also runs services to Central Africa and Madagascar.

Belgium found it essential to keep in close contact with her large overseas colony in the Congo Basin, and started a direct service between Brussels and

Léopoldville in 1935. The route was via Marseilles, Oran, across the Atlas Mountains to Colomb Béchar, over the Sahara to Gao, along the River Niger to Niamey (a route described in Chapter IV), and thence to Zinder, Fort Lamy, Coquilhatville and Léopoldville, with a recent extension to Elisabethville.

New Savoia-Marchetti planes are to be put on this service. Cruising at 217 m.p.h., they are amongst the fastest airliners in the world.

Sabena are at present planning—in co-operation with the Portuguese and South African Airways—to extend this airway to Cape Town.

In 1936, when I crashed my 'Gull' taking off from Colomb Béchar with a heavy load of petrol, I felt forlorn and stranded. Two days later, early in the morning as I was dressing, I heard the hum of an aeroplane. Hastily finishing my toilet, I raced outside and saw a plane gliding down to the aerodrome. I ran to make inquiries and was told it was Sabena's passenger plane on its way from the Belgian Congo to Brussels. It was due to leave in an hour after refuelling.

I could be home in two days! The prospect was entrancing and the idea no sooner born than adopted. I asked the pilot if he would wait for me, and with traditional Belgian courtesy he agreed.

One of the passengers turned out to be Tony Orta, Managing Director of Sabena, who was on his way home after personally examining the southern extremity of his long airline. No sooner did he learn of my troubles than he invited me to fly with them as a guest and did all he knew to make me more cheerful and comfortable. No wonder Belgium is proud of Sabena and its charmingly efficient manager.

The service to the Belgian Congo is run once a week, Sabena alternating with Air France, each operating once a fortnight. Sabena's service goes direct from Brussels to Marseilles and Oran, but when it is the turn of Air France, passengers are flown to Paris by Sabena, thence to Algiers by Air France, and into the Belgian Congo by Régie Air Afrique, finishing up at Brazzaville, the port on the French side of the Congo River, opposite Léopoldville.

Air services have made a tremendous difference to life in the Congo Basin, where surface transport is hopelessly slow on account of vast tracts of jungle interlaced with rivers where the currents are so rapid that vessels cannot navigate them. The white population of some twenty thousand people, centred mostly in the mining region of the Katanga, near the borders of Northern Rhodesia, are thus brought within a few days' journey of the capitals of Europe, and life has lost for them much of the terrifying isolation they must have felt, living as they do amidst a native population of over ten million.

South Africa's major airways system is South African Airways, which operates services to all four corners of the Union and beyond, from the grand new Rand airport at Germiston, Johannesburg. Besides this network of services—eight a week to Durban, four to Cape Town, two to Lourenço Marques, two to Windhoek, two to Bulawayo, one to Port Elizabeth, and one to Kisumu on the Equator—there are services from Durban connecting with the Imperial Airways Southampton–Durban service. In addition to the eight to the Rand, there are five to the Cape via East London and Port Elizabeth.

As well as these services within the Union, South African Airways connect the Rand with the Rhodesias and Kenya, following the same route formerly operated by Imperial Airways before flying-boats were introduced. The terminus of this line is Kisumu, 2336 miles, which is reached in three days from Johannesburg.

South African Airways has expanded very rapidly in the last few years. It was only formed in 1934, and by the beginning of 1938 all the chief centres of the Union were linked by regular services.

The man who did most to start an air service in the Union is Major A. M. Miller, whom I met in 1932 in Cape Town and who, incidentally, offered me a job with South African Airways, which I have often regretted not accepting. From 1920 onwards he worked incessantly to make South Africa air-conscious. In 1927 he made an air tour of the Union in a Moth plane, covering 2300 miles in eight days, and in 1929 began the first commercial service, when Union Airways flew the air mail from Cape Town to Johannesburg via Port Elizabeth and Durban.

The public quickly took to the air, as it was soon realised what a saving in time air travel afforded. The long climb from the coast to the 6000-feet high plateau of the interior restricts the speed of express trains, and natural climatic conditions are favourable to flying, the visibility usually being excellent and high winds rare.

Johannesburg, the largest city in South Africa and the centre of the gold-mining industry, is the head-quarters of South African Airways. The airport at Germiston, just outside Johannesburg, has just had £400,000 spent on improvements, which should make it one of the finest in the world.

To-day, South African Airways is the largest air concern in the Dominions, and second only to Imperial Airways in the whole Empire. New machines are on order and new services projected to include a 7000-miles airway from the Cape to the Congo, thence 2000 miles inland to Kenya, and finally southwards back to Cape Town.

Besides these commercial activities there is much virility in the flying-club movement in South Africa.

Wilson Airways Ltd., of Kenya Colony, founded and built up by Mrs F. K. Wilson, O.B.E., an efficient and indefatigable business woman of far-seeing vision and courage, is a company deserving of special mention. In 1929 they started with one aircraft, one pilot, and one engineer. It has steadily increased in scope and size, and to-day has not only taken over the operation of part of Imperial Airways land route, when the change was made to the coast route and to flying-boats, but has important mail contracts, and operates in addition a flying-training school at Nairobi.

Besides all these tasks, the Company serves the Tanganyika mining areas, carrying bullion to Kisumu for transhipment to the flying-boats for London, taking mining officials, machinery and motor-car spares as a return load. The Company also has an extensive charter service, providing planes for anything, from ambulance-carrying to ferrying hunting-parties to the abundant game reserves of the Ngorongoro Crater and the Serengetti Plains, and ferrying distinguished people and government officials from place to place over distances that, although short, would take days instead of hours by surface transport.

Wilson Airways and D.E.T.A., the Portuguese line, are the only companies in Africa using exclusively British aircraft. In South Africa German planes with American engines are mostly used.

Africa is a country made for aviation, not only because her vast distances need rapid transport to reduce their frightening size, and because whereat conditions are so regular in their variations that they can be charted in advance, but also because Africa hides incredible beauties and wonders of nature. The tourist to Africa can make wide use of air travel, and will find an aerodrome not far from most of the places he wants to visit.

If the Sahara attracts you, and you prefer not to take the cut-and-dried—very dried!—route following the trans-Saharan air- and motor-way via Reggan and Bidon Cinq (as described in Chapter IV), you can follow the less-known Hoggar route from Algiers, via In-Salah, through the wild grandeur of the Hoggar Mountains, towering to 9000 feet and rising sheer out of the sand. The scenery is indescribably beautiful. You can fly by Air Afrique to El Golea, loveliest of all the oases, on the edge of the Erg Occidental, where you get a wonderful view of yellow sand-dunes and waving palm-groves. The airway then goes to join the Tanezrouft route, and you can if you like make a sort of circular tour of the Sahara by flying over the Hoggar route to In-Salah and Tamanrasset, well known for the murder of Père Foucauld and the blood-soaked rebellions of the native Touaregs. To-day it is peaceful enough, and the climate is perfect at an altitude of 4593 feet. You then return via Reggan and Colomb Béchar to Oran. It is also possible to make an air tour of the oasis belt.

The best time of the year for the Sahara is between October and the end of April. In the summer the desert is much too hot for comfort. In the winter the weather is ideal for flying, with the sky always clear and the air dry and invigorating. The early morning, however, is the least bumpy time for flying, and I strongly recommend a start at dawn.

The Sahara is a beautiful country, infinite in its variation. Gorgeous sunrises give way to even more magnificent sunsets; cool, dark palm-groves make startling contrast with burning yellow sands, whilst graceful branches wave soft greenery against a hard blue sky ; majestic mountains rise sheer from a floor of shifting sand, and in unexpected places you stumble across splashing pools, sometimes filled with fish!

. . . . . .

A flight on Italy's airline will take you, via Cairo, across the Sudan plains into the mountainous country of Eritrea. The mountains rise higher and higher until you are flying over a tableland at an elevation of nearly 8000 feet. On the top you land at Asurara, 7800 feet high, where the clear cool air is most stimulating after the hot moist air of the plains.

The next stage to Addis Ababa is over some of the grimmest country imaginable, the uninhabited Dankalia Desert looking very like a piece of the moon as seen through a powerful telescope. Black craters seem to be scooped out of a hard earth stabbed with jagged crags and contrast fantastically with white salt lakes.

The aerodrome of Addis Ababa itself is 7200 feet above sea-level, and seems to be eternally guarded by flocks of kites which circle the town incessantly.

The Congo Basin offers a picture of steaming jungles, raging rivers, green-clad mountain ranges, and phantom-like craters, empty and bare or erupting clouds of steam and lava. At frequent distances are excellently run aerodromes of the Belgian and French airlines.

Neighbouring territory to the Belgian Congo on the south-east side is Rhodesia, world-famous as the country of the Victoria Falls, discovered by Livingstone in 1855.

Rhodesia is a wooded and well-watered country of gently rolling plains, swamps, and ridges of hills rising from 3000 to 8000 feet, through which flows the mighty Zambesi River, with its numerous tributaries.

The swamps are not the humid morasses generally associated with jungles, but grassy areas full of picturesque lagoons and islands, haunted by wild fowl and a rare type of antelope, the Sitatunga, whilst fish abound in the lakes and rivers.

As well as the indescribably beautiful Victoria Falls are scores of lesser waterfalls and cataracts, amongst them the towering Kalambo Falls near Abercorn, with a sheer drop of 704 feet, the home of the rare Marabou Stork, which nests precariously on ledges a hundred feet down the steep gorge.

Tanganyika has the highest mountain in Africa, the giant Kilimanjaro, 19,718 feet, crowned with about the only snow you will see in Africa—until you go right south to Cape Town, where you are in a more temperate zone.

Kilimanjaro is often called the 'watchdog of Nairobi,' which lovely city in Kenya Colony it guards from its majestic height.

Kenya possesses three valuable assets: the virility of a young colony; natural opportunities for air transport offered by its wide expanse; and ideal climatic conditions.

As for the Union of South Africa itself, you must go there to believe the ideal climate, lovely scenery, and modern civilisation which rubs elbows with native customs of immemorial times. Cape Town, nestling at the foot of Table Mountain, is a city which means a great deal to me. Twice have I waited there to take off on return flights to England, and once I passed through on a cruise I was taking for my health, visiting Port Elizabeth with its world-famous Snake Park and on to Durban, where I spent one of the happiest fortnights in my life at the home of a well-known big-game hunter, William A. Campbell, affectionately known as 'Wac' to all his friends. His lovely modern house stands on the top of the cliffs, sprayed by the breaking waves of the Indian Ocean which scatter their foam just the same on picturesque African kraals farther along the cliff-side.

At Cape Town you can go west of the city and plunge into the cold waters of the Atlantic, or you can go to the east and bathe in the warm seas of the Indian Ocean. A little way from Cape Town, on the edge of the Indian Ocean, is the palatial home of Sir Abe Bailey at Muizenberg.

The seasons in Cape Town are the exact opposite of those in England. Winter is our summer, and your Christmas dinner will probably be strawberries and cream.

The modern adventurer in Africa is treading historic trails. It is barely a century since this Dark Continent was illuminated by the courage and persistence of men like Livingstone and Stanley and many other explorers whose names will go down in history. However, the romantic past cannot overshadow the still romantic present, though ancient ghosts will crowd your trails, jungle drums still send their mysterious messages and strange legends of dark Africa lurk behind your newspaper.

CHAPTER VIII

AIRWAYS IN EUROPE, ASIA, AND THE FAR EAST

1. EUROPE

EUROPE to-day is criss-crossed with airways, literally flying everywhere, from north to south, east to west: over Switzerland's snowy peaks to drop a winter sports party on the ice of the lake at St. Moritz, 6000 feet high, from sunny Portugal and the sparkling Riviera, 'way north to the fishing-grounds of the Baltic, and even farther north along Norway's magnificent coast-line, into the Land of the Midnight Sun.

Wherever you may want to go in Europe, you may be sure to get there by air. All you have to do is to buy an Aerial A B C, or ring up your favourite touring agency for time-tables and fares. Excursion trips, cheap day and round-trip tickets, aerial cruises, season tickets, all are at your disposal on the airlines of Europe exactly the same as on the railroads.

BELGIUM is so small that it is difficult to keep inside her borders once you find yourself in a fast modern aeroplane! The longest distance from frontier to frontier is only 170 miles. Even so, there are several daily services between Brussels and Antwerp.

Her main, and world-famous, airline is Sabena, a name mercifully shortened from a long description which no one could possibly remember. The fast modern transport machines of this line not only connect Brussels with almost every country, but extend far southwards to link up her possessions in the Belgian Congo. American Douglas and Italian Savoia-Marchetti machines are mostly used by Sabena, and the line has a grand reputation for safety in spite of the thick blankets of fog and cloud which so often cover, but never damp, gay Belgium. (Belgium's Overseas Airways are described in Chapter VII.)

GERMANY'S main airline is Deutsche Luft Hansa, whose activities I have outlined in other chapters. Aviation under Government control has reached a high degree of perfection in Germany. Pilots are being trained in thousands amongst the youth of the country, who are first of all given a training in gliding before being passed on to power machines. Her planes and engines are as excellent as her pilots, and, unlike so many other countries, she does not need to go outside her own borders for her equipment. Her activities extend wellnigh all over the world: in North and South Atlantic, in China, in Russia, and in Africa.

The great national line of FRANCE is Air France, an amalgamation of five lines made in 1933. France has always been a country where the temperament of her pilots suits her for record-breaking on a spectacular scale, and in the long list of pioneering efforts French names hold a high percentage. Her Government, too, seems a grateful one, for famous names still surviving almost always figure in some important Government or military post, as, for example, Codos, Rossi, Costes, Detroyat. The lines of Air France operate some 23,000 miles of airways, and extend south-east to French Indo-China, south and south-west to Africa, Madagascar, and South America, besides which they serve every important city in Europe. The longest route is 9360 miles, from London to Santiago.

Her name, too, is in the front line of development in the South Atlantic and the Far East. Nearly three hundred South Atlantic crossings had been made by July 1938; the experience gained will be used on experimental North Atlantic services.

Air France use Marcel Bloch 220's on the Paris–London airway. Cruising at 200 m.p.h., they cover the 225-mile journey in 1 hour 15 minutes. On this shortest route of their vast network of airways, Air

France holds the commercial speed record of 51 minutes, and on the longest route (Paris–Santiago) mails were carried in a demonstration flight by Paul Codos in 2½ days. The schedule time of 4 days makes it the fastest long-distance airway in the world. Dewoitine 338's are used, cruising at nearly 200 m.p.h. These planes have also just been introduced on the Far East airway to Hong Kong, making the journey in six days. It is interesting to note that Air France calculate their safety record as being a loss of 0.002 passengers' lives per million passenger miles, which is far superior to the safety records of motor-cars. Air France now, like Imperial Airways, serve a complete lunch on the midday plane.

'L.O.T.' is the name of POLAND'S national air-line, linking Warsaw with many of the capitals of Europe and running a trunk route south-eastwards by way of Athens to Palestine. American Lockheed Electras are mostly used.

Poland's inhabitants take naturally to flying, having a buoyancy of temperament, mechanical aptitude, and spontaneous courage which particularly fit them to be pilots.

An interesting development in Poland is gliding, for which the Poles have a tremendous enthusiasm. They have made such headway that it is no uncommon thing for a would-be gliding pilot from this country to go to Poland for his or her training. Ballooning and the Light Aeroplane Club movement also are very strong in Poland.

I am a great admirer of the Polish pilot's gay and carefree spirit. Never shall I forget having a forced landing near Warsaw and turning over my Moth on a snow-covered ploughed field, breaking the undercarriage in the process. A military pilot from Warsaw came to my aid, righted the machine, tied up the undercarriage with string, and flew it away! 'It is nothing,' they say when you thank them, and they mean it.

NORWAY, SWEDEN, DENMARK, and the BALTIC all have their own air services, which not only link their capital cities with those of most others in Europe, but in the summer have a thriving tourist traffic. Norway offers the grand scenery of her fjords, snow-fields and icy peaks. Sweden displays an enchanting panorama of lovely lakes. Denmark presents the hospitable and gay city of Copenhagen; whilst the Baltic and Finland provide holiday delights of unexcelled bathing, fishing, boating and sightseeing amongst delightfully unspoilt people, in a land which is a picture of graceful forests and sparkling blue sea. In winter the aeroplane unlocks the icebound Baltic and brings freedom to the farthest-north republic of Finland.

CENTRAL EUROPE and the BALKAN LANDS are well served by air. In all these countries in normal times the tourist traffic is immense. I flew to Hungary once for a ' Magyar Pilota ' picnic, a meeting of private planes organised by the Hungarian Government, and never shall I forget the charm and grace of her people and the friendliness and gaiety of Budapest. Switzerland's Swissair operates fast Douglas planes between Zurich, Basle and London. The former Czecho-Slovakia was particularly adept at manufacturing light aeroplane engines. The 60 h.p. Walter Mikron is one of the best known. Last summer I flew hundreds of miles behind one in a tiny two-seater Tipsy plane and was delighted with its performance and reliability.

HOLLAND is a small country, but with so much water to impede surface transport that it is not surprising she has taken to air transport very eagerly. There are more internal air routes in Holland than in any other country of its size and population.

Judging from the enormous numbers of sightseers at Schipol airport at Amsterdam—as many as 334,000 in a year—and the hundreds who still clamour for joy-rides, it would seem that the Dutch are a very air-minded race.

Holland's world-famous airline K.L.M. reaches out to the far side of the world, as well as running the internal air services linking her cities with all parts of Europe. First country in Europe to use fast American transport planes to speed up their overseas airways, Holland has repeatedly set other countries the pace.

K.L.M. claims to be the oldest air transport company in the world and is not the result of any amalgamation of smaller companies, as is usually the case with such a large concern. K.L.M. was incorporated as a company on the 7th October 1919, under the direction of a young Dutch Flight-Lieutenant, Albert Plesman, who is to-day the Managing Director and a very good friend of mine. The position which K.L.M. holds to-day in world air transport must be attributed largely to his foresight and enterprise.

It was not till 1927 that the Dutch Government took a financial interest in the company, but since that date their progress has been rapid.

K.L.M. very early saw that aviation must be international, and an affair of co-operation rather than competition. They led the way in co-operating with other national air companies, and to-day run numerous services throughout Europe, Asia, Africa and America, in conjunction with the A.B.A. (Swedish Air Lines), D.D.L. (Danish Air Lines), D.L.H. (German Airways), Air France, S.A.B.E.N.A.

(Belgian Air Lines), and in the Far East, with the K.N.I.L.M. (Royal Netherlands Indies Airways), a sister company. The latter operates a network of airlines in Java, Sumatra, Borneo, with connections to British Malaya and the Philippines.

Three famous European services of the K.L.M. line are the 'Scandinavian Air Express,' the 'Blue Danube Air Express,' and the 'Rome Air Rapide,' which run several services daily to Stockholm (via Copenhagen and Malmo), Budapest (via Prague and Vienna), and Rome (via Frankfurt and Milan) respectively.

In the summer of 1934 a service was opened across the North Sea between Amsterdam and Liverpool, originally via Hull, later via Doncaster, and recently with a stop at Manchester.

Although small in size, Holland has valuable and extensive colonial possessions, and she has extended her genius on the high seas to the skies. The Netherlands East Indies are reached in six days from Amsterdam to Batavia via the summer route of Budapest—a distance of 8737 miles. In winter a slightly longer route is taken via Rome in order to avoid the bad weather of the mountains of Central Europe.

Holland's other air links are with her possessions in the West Indies, where her lines connect with

Pan-American's services. A project of the future is to connect the Netherlands East Indies with Manila, air-junction of Pan-American Airways in the Philippines. Passengers from the East Indies and from Australia will then be able to fly direct to Hong Kong, or even on to the United States via Manila and Honolulu.

Holland has many world-famous names amongst her K.L.M. pilots. Commander I. W. Smirnoff, a grand person as well as a marvellous pilot, and a well-known figure in Holland, where he has just published his reminiscences, piloted the first official passenger flight from Amsterdam to Batavia ten years ago last November, and has many record flights to his credit. I was lucky enough to have him as pilot on the K.L.M. plane which brought me home in 1934 after our misadventures in the England–Australia Air Race. We became firm friends during that trip, and I envied him his remarkable imperturbability no matter how bad the weather or how irritating the passengers.

Born in Russia, he learned to fly with the Russian Air Force. He escaped from Russia in the revolution and went to China, where he served with the British Army. He has had a most eventful life, packed with travel, adventures, and a variety of jobs. He finally became a naturalised Dutchman, and was awarded a medal for his services to aviation in the Netherlands.

K.L.M. entered a standard Fokker Douglas D.C. 2 twin-engined monoplane (Wright Cyclone 700 h.p. engines) for the Handicap Section of the famous air race from Mildenhall to Melbourne in October 1934. Piloted by K. D. Parmentier and J. J. Moll, two of K.L.M.'s veteran pilots, with a crew of four, three passengers, and 191 kgs. of mail, they won the handicap event with a time of 3 days 18 hours 17 minutes, coming in second in the race as a whole. This flight not only made the names of K.L.M. and her pilots world-famous, but attracted widespread attention to the Douglas airliner. There is little doubt that this type of machine dates its great popularity as an airliner outside the American frontiers to its outstanding success in this race. K.L.M. immediately ordered a fleet of them, and other nations soon followed suit.

'Tony' Fokker, the famous Dutch aircraft designer, had immediately recognised the potentialities of the Douglas planes and bought the concession to manufacture them in Holland. His own planes, of course, are world-famous.

Fokker, whom I know well, has one of the finest brains I have ever come across. His book, *Flying Dutchman*, of which I proudly possess an autographed copy, is packed with action, creative achievement and triumph, and is enlivened with his particular brand of dry, mischievous humour which makes him seem more like a naughty schoolboy than a sedate professor of aeronautics. Incidents of his boyhood I particularly liked are his explanation of his facility for passing examinations: 'Usually there were ten questions in an examination, eight of which could be systematically recorded. These I answered fairly correctly. The two informal questions, which demanded some study of the subject, I always answered a hundred per cent. wrong. My average was just enough to pass. I enjoyed the whole thing because it seemed a test of skill between me and the teachers. They failed to notice the black shutter operated by a tiny wire which was moved by the quiet motion of my body.'

When he had to stay indoors to write punishment lines, he whittled a piece of wood which would hold four pens—what he calls 'my first successful experiment with quantity production methods.'

One of the rules he often had to write was 'Time is money,' which gave him an idea. When he had to write the lines at home he called in some neighbour boys and hired them for a few cents to do the writing for him, whilst he went out to sail his boat or labour in the attic with his endless experiments.

He built a plane before he ever saw one in the air, taught himself to fly, and in Germany was the first pilot to loop the loop. Before the Great War of 1914 was declared, his odd-looking but 'inherently stable' monoplane was turned down by Russia, Italy, Holland and England. Two years later, England willingly offered a couple of million pounds to rectify that error, but Germany's answer was to make Fokker a German citizen, for he had just invented the synchronised machine-gun which revolutionised aerial warfare.

The end of the war found him twenty-eight years old, a multi-millionaire, but apparently without a country. When Germany ran red with revolution he smuggled out of the country into Holland several train-loads of planes, motors and accessories, capping this achievement by smuggling out his money as well.

He is a man of unbounded energy, tireless, who thinks sleep is a waste of time and makes up for it in odd naps anywhere, any time. With his great inventive genius is mixed an unusual amount of business acumen.

Some other famous names in K.L.M. are G. J. Geysendorffer and J. B. Scholte and Commander Fryns, all of whom have made many record pioneering flights for K.L.M. and to-day are amongst the 'Air Millionaires' (those with a million miles in the air to their credit).

TURKEY has a four-year air plan, drawn up last July to operate Turkish airlines. The 'Turk Kusu' (Turkish Air League) encourages air-mindedness among the young people particularly, and both gliding and private flying are enjoying a fashionable vogue. Turkish girls have cast aside the veil and are learning to fly. In nine Turkish gliding schools girls and boys are given free training, the most capable being selected for training in the Aviation School. Both men and women agree to serve the State for five years as instructors.

Turkey's main airways system is operated by Turkish State Airways, with headquarters at Ankara. British machines are mostly used.

ITALY'S contributions to aviation history are mainly on the engineering side. Her aeroplanes and engines are seen on many a foreign aerodrome; as fast as height and distance records are taken away from her she seeks to regain them; her knowledge of the aeroplane in warfare is increased by her experiences in Abyssinia and Spain; whilst spectacular record-flights take a front place in her programme of world propaganda.

The gallant Marshal Balbo's formation flight across the Atlantics will long be remembered.

According to his book, *My Air Armada*, translated from the Italian, he aimed to establish a ' permanent bond, if possible, with America's great band of aviators ' because he was greatly impressed by America's progress in technical and aeronautical achievement. He dropped the idea of solitary flights by individual aeroplanes because ' they would not entail the profound social and civil reactions ' of which he had been dreaming.

A mass flight to America was certainly a great ideal, and all credit must be given Italo Balbo for its conception and for translating the idea into glorious achievement.

As a preliminary experiment, a flight of Italian aeroplanes flew the South Atlantic on 17th December 1930. Forty-four men made this crossing and, elated by such a triumph, Balbo decided to go ahead with his more ambitious plans for the North Atlantic crossing.

It is not surprising that he had many set-backs before such a vast scheme came to fruition, but finally in 1933 he was ready, with a flight planned as Italy's glorious contribution to the impending Chicago International Exhibition.

On 1st July 1933, in command of 25 flying-boats carrying 115 men, Balbo took off from Orbetello, after years of hard work and careful preparation.

The outward route was over the Alps, across Europe, the British Isles, over the North Atlantic to Labrador and Canada, thence across Lake Michigan to Chicago, where they kept their date at the Exhibition.

(Arriving there myself a week or so later, I basked in their reflected limelight, enjoying 'the Balbo Suite' at the Drake Hotel in Chicago, and boasting of friendly cables exchanged with the genial Marshal.)

From Chicago the squadron flew to New York, and then came the return journey, using the more southern route via the Azores, Lisbon, Gibraltar, and the Mediterranean to the Lido of Rome, to a well-deserved public reception.

Only two mishaps, one at Amsterdam on the outward flight, and the other at the Azores on the homeward journey, marred the magnificence of this great mass flight which captured the imagination of the world.

1938 saw a formation flight of 6250 miles over the South Atlantic in twenty-four hours made by three Savoia-Marchetti bombers of the Italian Royal Air Force.

Italy, too, believes in training pilots first on gliders, and in the Air Force this preliminary training is compulsory.

Her main air company is the 'Ala Littoria,' which operates services linking all the principal cities of Italy, as well as lines to Sardinia, Athens, the island of Rhodes, Cadiz, Lisbon, Tripoli, and to all parts of Albania. During the summer this company also operates a line direct from Rome to Paris and London. Other international services (operated in conjunction with airlines of other countries) are those from Rome to Berlin, Prague, Vienna, and Budapest.

Italy now also has a line to Abyssinia to communicate with the newly acquired territories in Africa; several subsidiary services operate from Addis Ababa, linking outlying towns with the capital city.

2. Central Asia

Even Tibet the inaccessible is falling beneath the civilising cloak of aviation. If her ancient mysteries and sacred monasteries become open to conducted tours, where else is there left in the whole wide world where hidden romance can be found?

Surrounded by majestic Himalayan peaks, this wild country, however, still retains much of her aloofness, in spite of the efforts of the late Panchen Lama to modernise the country. Engaging an American to help him, he used aeroplanes to fly gold out of the country—millions of pounds' worth of gold which had been accumulating in the monasteries for centuries. Within the country itself gold has no real value, the Tibetans often burying nuggets in the ground in the belief that it is a plant.

Before he died, the 'Living Buddha' actually flew himself when he returned to Tibet. On a special throne of yellow cushions, which was prepared for him in the plane, he sat cross-legged in pleased serenity. Captain Hans Koester, well known for much valuable pioneer flying in China, was the pilot to fly the Lama back to his mountain monastery, Kumbum. To welcome him when he landed at the flying-ground at Sining came his priests, riding ponies and clad in golden helmets, women glittering in hand-carved jewellery, and his own private band! Dressed in Western uniforms and playing modern instruments, their music, even so, was far from tuneful to Western ears—or was it perhaps merely ultra-modern?

That immensely high plateau separated from the world by gigantic mountain chains and vast stretches of arid desert may yet, however, find its isolation violated by a future express airline between England and Australia, since the shortest route for such an airline passes directly over the centre of mysterious Tibet.

IRAN, formerly Persia, the inner fortress of the Moslem world, is a country where passions run as wild and naked as the savage terrain itself.

The present Shah has brought this ancient and turbulent country to the threshold of modern times, but even to-day, whilst many of the squalid villages have filling-stations and cinemas, yet the beautiful capital city of Teheran lacks a sewage system.

Riza Shah Pahlavi, despotic ruler of an enormous territory stretching from Turkey to Afghanistan, is a man of foresight, energy, and ambition, and every reform in Iran to-day can be traced directly to his acute brain, sharpened and influenced probably by a visit he once paid to Kemal Ataturk, a man he admired immensely.

Whilst he encourages aviation and has built an excellent airport at Teheran, yet his violent likes and dislikes once led him to cancel Germany's Luft Hansa air service[1] and prohibit our own Imperial Airways from flying over Persian territory except a narrow coastal strip along the Persian Gulf (one of the reasons why we have pushed ahead with our flying-boats landing on British waters). He allows the Dutch K.L.M. line to use Iran as a stepping-stone on their Holland–Dutch East Indies airway, although even this permission has to be renewed continually.

[1] This is again in operation at the moment.

Flying along the Persian Gulf on my way to Australia in 1930, I was impressed particularly by the gorgeous colours of the water and the rainbow-tinted saw-toothed ridges of bare chains of mountains inland, and for the solace of those who might complain of the Shah's treatment, I would say that it is decidedly more comfortable to be in a flying-boat over the waters of the Gulf than bumping about amongst mountain ranges, where a forced landing would have most unpleasant consequences.

3. The Far East

Everyone knows what is meant by the 'Far East'—Japan, China, Manchuria, and Asiatic Russia—yet it depends on which way we are looking at the globe whether these countries lie to the far east or to the far west. America is running an airway westwards across the Pacific to China; we are running one eastwards round the globe to meet at the same place.

It is an age-old axiom that civilisations follow the sun, *i.e.* westwards. America is the New World of to-day. We are the Old. Further westwards from America is the 'Far East.' Is it possible that the Air Age can herald the first glimmerings of the dawn of a new civilisation in the far west, or 'far east' if you prefer it? I think it is very possible.

What is the New World, as we term it to-day? Simply a modern veneer covering a civilisation predating that of the Old World as we term it to-day. Cannot a similar thing happen again?

The 'yellow nations' are beginning to realise the power of their teeming millions. Profiting by modern methods of education, they employ an age-old wisdom to improve on them to their own advantage. Japan is slowly but surely absorbing China—or, as some think, China is slowly but surely absorbing Japan. In either event, the two nations, if closely linked, and perhaps some day supported by Asiatic Russia, will have the mighty power of an elephant directed by brains of Oriental cunning with all the advantages of modern science and knowledge.

All three countries have profited greatly by utilising Western inventions, and have even gone to the extent of inviting American and German experts over to organise their airways, train their pilots, and give them advice on all aeronautical matters. So far as aeroplanes and equipment are concerned, they mainly use German and American products, although Russia is fast becoming an important centre of aircraft construction.

China is not only linked with the United States by Pan-American and with the British Isles by Imperial Airways, but Russia, France, and Holland all have their own air connections with Hong Kong. Within China itself are two national airways, one operated by Pan-American Airways and the other by German interests. Both are based at Shanghai, use modern equipment and radio, and have excellent Chinese pilots. In peace-time these lines operate with regularity and serve the populous Great Plain of China and the lowlands of her three great rivers. In these days of war, even as I write, the map of this part of the world is rapidly changing, as port after port in China falls into Japanese hands. China is desperately trying to keep open her 'back door' communications via Burma, and is running a new mail and passenger service between Chungking and Rangoon. China has one natural advantage over Japan, and that is that her people take more readily to flying than do the Japanese. It is, too, a country of vast distances, mighty geographical barriers, and swarming millions, so air transport is obviously the key to China's future progress.

JAPAN has a great need of airlines to bridge her main cities, separated as they are by high mountain ranges and oceans. Japan Air Transport operates internal routes within her islands, whilst other lines link her with the mainland of Korea and thence with Manchukuo. Modern 'Miss Japan' acts as the perfect air hostess.

In 1931 I flew from England to Japan by way of Russia, Siberia, Manchuria (as it was then), Korea, and the Japan Sea, covering the distance in ten days. This route has not been followed up as a through air-line, although sectionally it is operated by the air-lines of the various countries over which it passes.

Japan is fully alive to the vital importance of air transport. In her war with China she is gaining invaluable experience of the aeroplane as a weapon of destruction, but she is, at the same time, planning to use the aeroplane constructively to her future gain.

At the moment she holds the world's record for distance in a closed circuit, which unfortunately beats, in actual length, our own long-distance record of the Vickers-Wellesleys. She encourages her pilots to make individual record flights, if possible in Japanese-made machines. Is it possible that the ' writing on the wall ' can already be seen in the recent announcement that a new air service is to be opened by Japan from Tokyo to the Pelew Islands, a mere 1500 miles from Darwin and Port Moresby in Papua ? This means that the Japanese will have an air base within bombing range of the mainland of Australia, whilst conquest of New Guinea would be only too easy.

RUSSIA is definitely a country to be reckoned

with, so far as aviation is concerned. This country, of vast size but of one political unit, covering one-seventh of the land surface of the globe and supporting a widely scattered population of some 170 millions, is obviously crying out for air services to give it unity and the U.S.S.R. herself has not been slow to realise this.

Foreign experts have been commissioned to give advice, money has been lavished by the Government, and 'shop-window dressing' in the shape of record-flying and exploration has been arranged and financed by the State itself.

All important towns in both European and Asiatic Russia are linked by air, but the organisation is by no means so excellent as that of the United States, even though the mileage flown is second only to that of America.

Russia's most noteworthy contribution to aviation is her Polar exploration work over the 'top of the world.' Experimental flights have already been made with a view to running a service between U.S.S.R. and the U.S.A. via Siberia, for which purpose a base camp was established at the North Pole in 1937.

The story of this camp in the ice-floes of the Arctic, and of the Russians' subsequent flights making use of the data collected, is one of the most adventurous in aviation history. Every single item of equipment was flown to the camp by Russian aeroplanes, enough to last for a year. To test the ice-floes for landing, heavy cannon-balls were dropped, and brightly-coloured powder scattered to find the direction of the wind.

Previous to this, many flights had been made in the Polar region, notably by Amundsen, Lincoln Ellsworth, 'Dick' Byrd, Floyd Bennett, Sir Hubert Wilkins, and others, but no one as yet had used the Pole as a non-stop air route between East and West. On 20th June 1937, the Russian ANT-25, with a single 950 h.p. engine, landed at Vancouver with a crew of three, after a 'great circle' non-stop flight from Moscow of 5288 miles in 63 hours 17 minutes. They passed the North Pole twenty miles from the camp.

Later in the year, in July, another plane identical to the first covered the same route, this time landing at San Jacinto in California, after a flight of 6,295.6 miles, lasting 62 hours 17 minutes. Again three Russian pilots stepped triumphantly out of the aeroplane, announcing that they had enough petrol left to fly several hundred miles farther, but that their orders had been to fly to the United States, so here they were.

Russia was now optimistically forecasting regular

commercial services between Moscow and the United States by way of the North Pole, but the very next attempt was destined to shake this hope. In August, Sigismund Levanevsky, known as the 'Russian Lindbergh,' left with five companions in a huge four-engined monoplane for America. Beyond a radio message soon after they had left to say they were having trouble with their radio set, nothing further was ever heard of them, in spite of widespread search.

There is little doubt, however, that it is merely a matter of time before the North Pole will become merely a stepping-stone on a great northern airway. So much has been learnt of Arctic flying, by Pan-American with their service in Alaska, by Canadian Airways up in the frozen north, and by the Russians in their development by aeroplane of their vast tracts of land lying north of the 62nd parallel, and by numerous individual record and exploration flights over and around the North Pole, by day and by night, in winter as well as in summer, that the difficulties to-day can be said to be less technical than political. The route is such a rational one, being the shortest way of linking up the cities of the northern hemisphere, that its realisation can definitely be forecast as a future development.

Moscow is linked to Western Europe by an airline operated jointly by the U.S.S.R. State Air Lines, 'Aeroflot,' and the Swedish airline company, 'A.B. Aerotransport.' Planes leave Moscow daily for Riga and Stockholm, whence connections can be made with K.L.M. (Dutch) and D.L.H. (German) airlines to London and Berlin.

Russians are adepts at parachute jumping. At any aviation meeting it is a familiar sight to see a mass parachute jump of some hundred people. Their military experts maintain that it is possible to drop large numbers of troops by parachute and thus occupy a territory more quickly than by actually landing the planes themselves.

In Russia there are parachute towers in many of the public parks, and ordinary citizens are encouraged to use them. It is regarded as an amusing form of sport, but it has its practical side too, in that it trains people to use a parachute properly, and safe landings from these towers are comparatively simple. In the United States such towers are used for training purposes, and the French services are also installing some.

There is no doubt whatsoever that Russian aviation has made tremendous strides in recent years. Not only are her pilots extraordinarily skilful and tough—as is proved by the numerous long-distance flights they have successfully carried out—but her home-constructed planes, engines, and equipment are of high and reliable performance, as all must admit who judge by results.

Under the guidance of her ' Air Ministry '—the ' Ossoaviakhim '—she spends unlimited time, money and energy on making herself one of the foremost countries in the aviation world, and she is rapidly succeeding.

CHAPTER IX

THE THREE AMERICAS

1. THE UNITED STATES

IN 1933, whilst waiting for a new aeroplane to arrive when the ill-fated *Seafarer* had crashed at Bridgeport after crossing the North Atlantic, I was invited by Trans-Continental & Western Air, one of America's main airlines, to cross the continent as co-pilot on one of their ordinary schedule runs. Such an opportunity was too good to be missed. I was in the land of opportunities, a country where a woman is given a job according to her qualifications and not her sex, where new ideas are tried out and not just pigeon-holed. I accepted with alacrity.

Dressed in a natty blue suit and proudly wearing the T.W.A. badge on my beret, I climbed into the cockpit of a three-engined Ford on a certain fine summer morning. In those days, cruising along at about 110 m.p.h., it took a good twenty-four hours to cross the continent from coast to coast. Passengers had the option of making the whole journey ' non-stop ' (*i.e.* so far as they were concerned : the plane actually landed about fourteen times, was changed half-way across, and pilots changed each quarter-section) or staying the night at Kansas City and continuing on their way in daylight. There was, therefore, night-flying even in those days, but passengers did not then have the luxury of sleeping-berths.

This trip gave me an intimate picture of the working of an American airline. In later years I have done a great deal of flying all over the States, both on the passenger lines and by private plane, and I feel I can say with some experience and authority that America has taught us a lot about running airlines and building passenger-carrying planes. Commercial flying in the States is more fully developed than in any other country in the world, one reason being that her population of some hundred and twenty-six million people has made it well worth while to run efficient services for their benefit. Another reason is that the distances between towns is great enough to make air transport quicker than any other means, yet not so great that the line must be unremunerative when the traffic cost-of-construction ratio is considered. A third reason undoubtedly is that it is far easier from every point of view to run an airway within a country which is one political unit, rather than through a series of countries with artificial barriers of frontier, differences of language, customs and exchange, and the incessant worry of maintaining diplomatic relations; whilst a fourth reason is that, very early in their history (in 1926) the Bureau of Air Commerce took the enterprising step of financing ground equipment, and substantially subsidising the main airlines.

In 1933, years ahead of other countries, America was flying regular schedules at night, producing and using 'blind-flying' instruments and with extremely efficient radio services. On my trans-continental flight I flew by day with ear-phones over my ears listening to the steady purr which told me I was on my course. If I wandered to one side or the other a difference in note in my ears immediately warned me. Every hour a weather report was automatically sent out over a second radio set, whilst a switch-over key enabled us to talk to ground stations or with other aircraft in flight.

In clouds and fog a 'sensitive' altimeter (sensitive down to the last few feet from the ground owing to a second hand making the round of the 'clock' for each hundred feet, as well as the ordinary hand marking every thousand feet of altitude) and artificial horizon and gyro compass (all instruments designed in America especially for bad weather flying), made us independent of sight of the ground.

At night the route was marked by flashing beacons, with special ones to indicate aerodromes, each main airport having its own Morse signal.

Three years later Eastern Air Lines, another important airline operating mainly from New York southwards to Georgia and Florida, invited me to fly on a test flight to New Orleans. They were trying out the latest Douglas airliner. Breakfasting bright and early in New York, we boarded the plane at Newark airport, flew smoothly and incredibly swiftly from north to south of the United States and back again in time for dinner, a total distance of almost 3000 miles in fifteen hours.

Up in the pilot's cockpit, I gazed around fascinated at a hundred knobs and switches, yet found that the plane was easier to fly than the old three-engined Ford. Able to talk without raising our voices, flying high above the clouds and bad weather with no intermediate landings to waste time, no bumps to make us feel air-sick, nothing to see except clouds and sky, so that we could not appreciate our speed of over 200 m.p.h., it was difficult to believe that one minute we were over New York in the cold of a winter's morning and, a little more than seven hours later, were basking in southern sunshine.

The return seven hours convinced us that something will have to be done to amuse passengers on such uneventful flights where you see nothing, feel nothing, and merely sit. You can't even sit and think at great heights, as you feel a certain amount of inertia due to lack of oxygen and lowered air pressure. I have often recommended that passengers should be given a pill at starting, and awakened at the end of the journey!

To-day the United States is a vast network of airlines. From east to west across the continent, a distance of about 2600 miles, three airlines operate in mutual co-operation. To avoid cut-throat competition, the three lines take slightly different routes so that all the cities within a fairly wide band across the continent are served by one airway or the other.

Thus T.W.A. operates the 'middle' route with two lines, one, the shorter, of 2557 miles between New York and Los Angeles via Pittsburgh, St Louis, Kansas City, and Albuquerque; and the other, of 2583 miles, through Chicago and Kansas City. Douglas twin-engined planes are used, cruising at speeds of over 200 m.p.h., and the coast-to-coast schedule is approximately seventeen hours, rather less on the trip east with prevailing winds, and a little more in the opposite direction. Night services use planes with sleeping berths, and by day there are 'ordinary' and 'de luxe' services, the latter being slightly faster, more comfortable, and of course more expensive. Enormous four-engined Boeing machines were being built in 1938, and T.W.A. are experimenting with high-altitude, sub-stratosphere aircraft to operate at 30,000 feet above storms and turbulent air.

When I flew on the T.W.A. line in 1933, I remarked to the General Manager when I got back that it was such a pity we flew within twenty-five miles of the Grand Canyon and could not see it. I had a longing to see this remarkable 'Wonder of the World,' and felt certain that to fly over it would be an attraction to passengers. It is significant, therefore, that T.W.A. to-day advertise their line as the airline which flies right over the Grand Canyon and the Painted Desert. The Grand Canyon is certainly well worth seeing. I once went all the way just to see it and intended spending the night there only. I stayed two months, and flew passengers 'way down inside the Canyon amongst its fantastic mountains and valleys—but that is not a story for this book. The T.W.A. line also flies over Boulder Dam, that marvellous piece of engineering which has been built at a cost of 165,000,000 dollars to dam up the waters of the Colorado River.

The trans-continental line to the North of T.W.A.

is United Air Lines, the oldest established airline in the States. This line also operates twin-engined Douglas planes, and flies from New York to San Francisco via Chicago. Up till 1937 Boeings were used, and well do I remember a flight made some years ago by night on this line across the dreaded Allegheny Mountains, noted for their habitual bad weather. Scarcely a sight did we get of the ground—or of the sky—between Chicago and New York. When we landed safely the pilot and I exchanged one glance which needed no words. We understood perfectly. To-day the flight has fewer hazards, not because the weather or the mountains have changed, but because we know better how to conquer them.

United Air Lines serve the densely populated regions of the Mississippi Basin and the 'Middle West.' It is also the trans-continental line which takes passengers on to join the Pacific Airways from San Francisco to the Far East.

The most southerly trans-continental line is American Airlines. Using Douglas machines, they fly between New York and Los Angeles daily, one express service making the flight with only three stops, and another with four. These two services are by night and the plane is equipped with sleeping berths.

The crew on all these planes consists of the chief

pilot, first officer (who is also the radio operator), and a stewardess. America is the country for air stewardesses, who appear almost as romantic in current films and fiction as the pilot himself. Intelligent, because they must be first-class nurses and well educated; attractive, and of good figure, because they must not weigh more than 115 lb. and must be of a type able to soothe and distract a sick or nervous passenger; and surrounded by the glamour of the air, it is not surprising that the marriage rate with them is higher than in any other profession. (K.L.M. is the only other important airline regularly employing 'air hostesses.')

It is a significant fact that American airlines tend to concentrate on the smaller, high-speed twin-engined plane rather than on the multi-engined type, the reason being that they believe frequency of service pays the best. Whilst larger planes are being ordered by some companies for express non-stop services, they still refuse to sacrifice manœuvrability to mere size.

American Airlines also have a service linking up New York with Montreal, which assumes a new importance in view of the proposed London–Montreal airline across the North Atlantic.

Eastern Air Lines, the President of which is Captain 'Eddie' Rickenbacker, famous War ace and a great personal friend of mine, who has more than once taken me for a ride on his airline, run services chiefly from New York to the south and south-east, to picturesque Florida, 'playground of the millionaires,' and to Georgia of 'Chain-gang' fame (where I actually saw black-and-white-striped convicts at work on the aerodrome at Atlanta. It is no uncommon sight in Georgia). The terminal airports are at New Orleans and Miami, Pan-American's stepping-off port for her giant 'Clipper' services to the West Indies and South America. Eastern Air Lines has a fine record of safety, and was recently awarded a Certificate of Special Commendation from the National Safety Council. The commendation states in part:

> Winner of the First Aviation Safety Award covering the operating period, including the years 1930-1936, Eastern Air Lines increased its safe operating record during the year 1937 to include approximately 180,000,000 passenger miles without a passenger fatality.

In other chapters I have described something of Pan-American's vast organisation.

America has numerous other airlines, and it is probably safe to say that not a town of any size is without its airport. Besides airline flying, there is a tremendous amount of taxi and charter work, and daily 'commuting' to and from business is a regular feature of American life. Never shall I forget being invited for the week-end to the late Dick Hoyt's (a well-known American financier) luxurious home on the Hudson River. Meeting him at his Wall Street office on the Friday afternoon, we walked the short distance to the quay at the end of the street, where we found his four-seater Loening Amphibian tied up all ready. Climbing on board, Dick settled himself in the pilot's seat, pressed the self-starter, and skilfully took off amongst what seemed like hundreds of boats of every shape and size.

In no time we were in the air, but right ahead of us was a bridge. 'He'll never get enough height to climb over it,' I remember thinking nervously, but he kept straight on and went—underneath! He never climbed much higher, as visibility was bad, and we just flew a few feet off the water with the comfortable feeling we could land anywhere.

In about twenty minutes' time he throttled back the engine, glided down, landed smoothly on the water, turned a mysterious handle as he was taxi-ing towards the sandy shore, and, lo and behold! we emerged from the water like a huge duck with its legs down and climbed up the shore on two wheels, where we parked ourselves safely and climbed out high and dry to walk across to a pretty white house nestling among cool dark trees. That's what I call finding an aeroplane really useful for business, and it is used that way a great deal in the States.

America has incidentally made a good job of 'sign-posting the air.' Every town and city has its name painted on the gasometer, or railway line. In 1936 the Bureau of Air Commerce employed four well-known women pilots to arrange for this to be done.

2. Central and South America

Although actually it was Air France which operated the first airline in South America in 1927 by extending their South Atlantic line from Natal to Buenos Aires, yet the story of air transport in this country of rolling plains, impenetrable jungles and mighty mountain ranges is largely one of Pan-American Airways.

In 1927 Air France were just inaugurating their air link with the rich cities of South America, making the actual Atlantic crossing by boat. On reaching the far side, mails were transferred to waiting planes and flown down the coast to Rio de Janeiro and Buenos Aires.

In 1929 another line was run to Santiago in Chile, crossing the barrier of the Andes. The German airline, Deutsche Luft Hansa, to-day operates between

Buenos Aires and Santiago, and a South American airway called ' Aéroposta Argentina ' links up many busy mutton and wool ports in the sheep-rearing districts with wealth-producing oilfields in Patagonia. The Company is subsidised by the Argentine Government and uses Junkers machines.

Practically the whole of the rest of air transport in South America is run by Pan-American Airways and its associated companies, and the routes they cover are amongst the most beautiful, interesting and wealthy in the world.

Competition for airline operation over these rich areas has been, and still is, fierce, but Pan-American are now so well entrenched and give such excellent service that it is doubtful whether other countries have any chance to compete.

A glance at the map, showing over 50,000 miles of air routes covered by this famous company, indicates how strong are the aerial bonds between the three Americas, the West Indies, the Far East, Bermuda, and Alaska away north, whilst across the North Atlantic the airway is tentatively dotted in. A service to New Zealand is also projected.

Miami, in Florida, is Pan-American's ' aerial gateway ' to the south. From this miniature seaside skyscraper city huge flying-boats leave several times a day for Nassau, tiny pleasure island sparkling like a diamond in lilac-tinted sea ; for the colourful lands of the West Indies on alternative routes, by east or west coast-line, or directly across the 600 miles of blue Caribbean Sea, on to South America, along the age-old routes of Columbus, and eastwards through Mexico up to San Francisco, whence airways radiate to the Far East and will shortly extend to our own Dominion of New Zealand.

Airlines link the twenty-one capitals of the twenty-one South American Republics and cover almost the whole of their territory so fabulously rich in minerals, oils and fertile lands. Some lines Pan-American operate direct, whilst others are directed by Pan-American but actually run by the Republics of Central and South America, Mexico and Cuba, amongst them being the well-known ones of 'Panair,' 'Pan-American-Grace Airways,' Peruvian Airways, and Columbian Airways (S.C.A.D.T.A.).

All kinds of planes are in service, right up to the huge four-engined ' Clipper ' ships of the Caribbean Sea ' laboratory,' from the use of which on this 600-mile crossing much of great value has been learnt and passed on to the Pacific and Atlantic routes.

The tale of conquest of hundreds of miles of open sea, of vast areas of unexplored jungle in the unknown interior of Central America, of struggles with four-mile-high mountain peaks, is one of fascinating interest, and flying to-day along these now docile airways leaves nothing to be desired in romance and enchantment.

Whether you decide to make a pleasure cruise of the West Indies, Central and South America by taking a round-trip ticket on one of the 'Air Cruises' arranged by Pan-American Airways at an inclusive price, or whether you merely have to go on prosaic business, you will find that travelling by air will not only save you time and money, but will give you food for thought, entertaining material for conversation, and entrancing mind-pictures for many a year to come.

Let us suppose that you have a month to spare and decide on an air cruise to the Argentine via the east coast of South America, returning by the west coast, the Canal Zone and Mexico.

You can arrange your trip as you like, either staying several days overnight at the places which appeal to you the most, or you can push through as fast as you please, taking six days or six weeks to reach Buenos Aires.

Leaving Dinner Key airport in Miami early in the morning, your first halt for the night is San Juan in Porto Rico. If it amuses you, however, you can stop first at Port au Prince in Haiti, home of 'Voodoo' and the Citadel of the Black King

Christophe. This mighty monument to the monstrous arrogance of a black man seems to be built into the living rock, terrace upon terrace rising up from the boulders in a sort of mad dream, making a silhouette of a fortress which stands out against a hard blue sky in tremendous unreality.

Heavy iron cannon are actually there, and the only way to account for their presence is to believe the stories told. Every piece of enormous masonry is stained with the blood of slaves and oxen, and lying in a lime-pit in its midst is the body of the king himself, surrounded by the black ghosts of the Dukes of Lemonade and Marmalade he created in his crazy reign.

San Juan presents a totally different atmosphere. Bright and cheerful is its carefree life, a life of dancing in jasmine-scented moonlight, and of beautiful women, clad in the latest Paris gowns, wandering down silvery aisles on the arm of some brightly decorated uniform.

If this 'petite Paris' does not keep you, you can fly away the next morning, past many a tiny island rich in beauty and history; St Thomas, where the authentic Bluebeard's castle is now a modern hotel; a Dutch town nestling in the crater of an extinct volcano, poking its nose out of the sea; over Antigua, where Nelson fitted out the ships for

Trafalgar; past Mont Pelée, the volcano that utterly destroyed 40,000 people in Saint Pierre, to Martinique where Napoleon's Josephine was born, on to Port of Spain in Trinidad in the British West Indies, and discover afresh this green island paradise unearthed by Columbus in 1498 on his third voyage to the New World. The tropical city of Port of Spain boasts some of the finest hotels in the West Indies—with huge canopied beds made twice a day, for everyone enjoys a siesta in the afternoon! Trinidad, a ' chip ' off South America, is a colourful mixture of all the islands of the West Indies, having a little of each in its complex personality. The island has passed through many hands, finally being taken by the British near the beginning of the nineteenth century.

Separating Trinidad from the coast of Venezuela is the estuary of the great Orinoco River, an area full of legend and mystery. El Dorado has definitely been located in the upper regions of the Orinoco, and many are the tales of the adventures befalling travellers into the interior, of white men lost in the jungle whose ghosts reach out long snaky arms to catch you, and the like.

Next you fly over the Guianas—British, Dutch and French, in that order. Miles of mud greet you as you sight the South American coast and the pilot searches round the wide, yellow Demerara river for a safe landing place. Georgetown in British Guiana is famous for its Demerara sugar, and your memory of this part of the world will probably be of this haunting smell, and of the almost intolerable sticky heat and rotting damp.

Paramaribo is the alighting place in Dutch Guiana, and after this stop you will probably be all agog to get a glimpse of Devil's Island, near to which you pass on your way to Cayenne, of 'red pepper' fame (and as hot!), in French Guiana. In the distance (it is forbidden to fly over them) you see three tiny islands, bare and sweltering in the tropic sun, which constitute France's penal settlement. Prisoners on parole are to be seen at the Cayenne landing stage, where they are allowed to pick up a few pence by doing odd jobs.

You are now nearing Brazil and begin to feel you are really in South America proper. Your landing at Belem, capital of the Brazilian state of Para, brings you amongst real South American people. You have passed over the Equator and are close to the huge gaping mouth of the Amazon, down which there is now an airline opening up a thousand miles of virgin forest to Manáos, and even pushing on another eight hundred miles beyond to Rio Branco, an important city at the eastern edge of the northern Andes.

Very few people fly this route just for the fun of it, but if you like to fancy yourself an explorer you can sit back in comfort and follow the winding of the fabled Amazon from safely on high.

Down below you will see tightly packed masses of trees, so thickly laced with dark undergrowth and liana vines that not a glint of sunshine can penetrate to the rotting earth. Sluggishly crawling in and out is the yellow river, 180 miles wide, choked up with mud and greedy swamps.

Back on your circular tour *en route* for Rio, you land first at Pernambuco, a port from which South American cotton, of as fine a quality as any produced in the world, is exported in ever-increasing quantities, to alight next at São Paulo, the coffee capital of Brazil. From here, an hour and a half's flight brings you to Rio de Janeiro, the fairy city of Brazil.

Rio is a glowing city of incomparable charm, and it is a safe bet to forecast that you will certainly decide to spend as long as possible at the internationally known Copacabana Palace Hotel, from the balconies of which you can gaze at the beauties of Rio spread out enticingly before your eyes, from the creamy beach with its smart striped umbrellas, out to the jewelled islands dotted in the glittering ocean, back to the Sugar Loaf dominating the landlocked harbour and over a scene of perpetual gaiety which is the city of Rio itself.

If you can tear yourself away from Rio—and you assuredly won't if it's Carnival time—you can continue on your way to Buenos Aires, that third largest city of the New World set in a select circle of sophistication in the midst of vast plains and rolling 'pampas.'

The capital of the Argentine is smart, modern, and immense, and 'Business first and last' appears to be its watchword. Business men throng the hotels, the streets, the clubs and buildings, and the atmosphere is busy and thoroughly cosmopolitan. The climate is healthy and pleasant, and you will find plenty here to interest you.

When you are tired of sightseeing, fashionable shops, and cocktail parties, you can wing your way onwards, taking a short-cut across the 'tail' of the continent—an area, incidentally, of some ten million acres of land that have never been explored—and look ahead to the vast Andes separating you from an utterly different world beyond.

Flying from Buenos Aires to Mendoza, at the foot of the Andes, you get an excellent bird's-eye view of the immensity of the Argentine 'campo,' the largest level plain in the world. Cattle graze in thousands, but even so are lost in this vast land, and every now and then you pass over a ranch or station which might equally be in Texas or Queensland.

Mendoza, watered from the Andes, is called 'the Garden of the Andes,' or the 'Argentine California,' and is literally an oasis of abundant fruit and flowers in a desert of coarse grass and scrub. Earthquakes are common here, and half a century ago the town was completely destroyed, with ten thousand people buried in the ruins.

Towering over Mendoza are the four-mile-high Andes, their snow-capped peaks decked in woolly caps of cloud.

The luxuriously equipped plane, with temperature regulated to suit the passengers, climbs steadily towards this tremendous barrier. The monsters give the illusion of advancing towards you and you have the feeling that you are gaining nothing in height, yet they approach you in leaps and bounds. At last they are on you, and you find yourself actually flying *through* them, through a pass with rocky sides seemingly so near in the clear air that you could reach out and touch them, yet in reality they are miles away.

Mount Aconcagua, 23,000 feet, is the giant of them all and remains monarch of all he surveys, looking down in icy disdain on your puny efforts to humble him.

On the border between Argentine and Chile you may see a huge stone figure of Christ, set up to mark peaceful agreement between the two countries, and within an hour of leaving Mendoza you will find yourself gliding down to land at Santiago, the capital of Chile. Before the aeroplane spanned the Andes, the journey across by train took a day and a half.

Santiago is a pleasant city, full of agreeable people radiating health and the 'cleanness' seemingly given them by the pure air of the Andes. It is surrounded by agricultural country, groves of fruit-trees and gardens. As you fly north, however, this delightful country gives place to deserts where it has not rained for a thousand years.

Northern Chile has very valuable natural mineral deposits, chief amongst them being nitrate of sodium. Northern Chile also exports 90 per cent. of the world's supply of iodine, which is a by-product of the nitrate industry. Copper is mined in the mountains of Northern Chile, which climb to 16,000 feet and form another of the obstacles which Pan-American have had to overcome.

Homeward bound, you land at Tacna in Peru, where you see surrounding the aerodrome white sand-dunes glistening with nitrate deposits. Peru is steeped in history and story, and still wears to-day its mantle of conquest like something tangible. It was the first country of South America to be conquered by the Spanish 'conquistadores,' and the ancient Inca Indians have never outgrown their amazement at the greed of the white men for silver and gold. Still to-day they mine it for the white man, or fashion it into ornaments and trinkets which they sell for next to nothing, as they have never realised, even after all these centuries, the value we place on gold and silver.

Still in Peru, we climb up 8000 feet into the coastal Andes, to land at Arequipa on one of the highest landing grounds in the world. Very, very old, and quaintly Spanish, Arequipa is a lovely gem of a city, guarded by three snow-capped volcanoes, of which El Misti is the most beloved by Arequipa's romantic inhabitants. This city, with its barred Moorish houses, ancient Spanish cathedral, and lovely hand-wrought ironwork, will probably tempt you, with its delicate charm and fascinating Inca legends, to delay your flight and explore its delights.

Lima, the 'City of Kings,' is the capital of Peru and was the original capital of all South America. It is the most truly Spanish of all South American cities and speaks pure Castilian Spanish. Perpetually hanging over Lima is a cloud-bank which brings moisture to the ground even though it rarely rains.

Climbing up through this layer of cloud, you will emerge above what looks like a level sea with sharp-pointed islands piercing the surface. These are the tops of very high mountains, and over these you fly northwards, over Inca ruins, sugar-cane plantations, and thousands of oil wells, on to the Canal Zone, making one brief stop at Guayaquil in Ecuador on your way.

You are now in Central America, flying over Columbia. From your vantage-point in the sky you have a grand view of the Panama Canal, and in half an hour you travel from the Pacific to the Atlantic, watching the mighty locks below and wondering about the ships of every nation and of every type which rub shoulders in the intimate friendship of the Canal.

You land at Cristobal, at the Atlantic entrance to the Panama Canal, and then, in fast Douglas land-planes, hurry on through Costa Rica, Nicaragua, the largest of the Central American republics, to Guatemala, the most progressive, where volcanoes destroyed Antigua, the former capital, and made of its ruins one of the most interesting villages in Central America. In Guatemala are evidences of very old civilisations, pre-dating even the Aztec empire and the Mayan civilisation.

And so on to Mexico, to my mind as fascinating

as any country in the world. Everywhere are historic ruins of long-dead cities, whilst Mexico City itself presents an amazing contrast of picturesque old and new, but both old and new are always Mexican and hold a flavour of something 'different,' which attracts art-lovers from the whole world over.

If you can ever tear yourself away from this treasure-store of the Americas, you can take a plane from Mexico City to anywhere in the world.

CHAPTER X

GLIMPSE INTO THE FUTURE

IT is good fun to guess 'What next ?' To speculate on how fast and how high we shall fly to-morrow ; to imagine a day when planes are as cheap and plentiful as motor-cars ; to dream dreams of rocket flights to the planets for week-ends in a new world; and to wonder if the day will ever come when the aeroplane will be the tool of peace and progress and not a weapon of destruction.

New and more advanced designs are germinating in the brains of plane and engine designers so soon as the old ones are pinned to the drawing-board. Scientists are busy edging back the limit-line of impossibility. One-time wonders are everyday commonplaces.

Rather than paint a Wellsian picture of 'Things to Come,' I will try to indicate the more immediate future, something that is within our reach and which most of us will live to see, because, attractive as some of the forecasts are of speeds of a thousand miles an hour and round the world in twenty-four hours, I am afraid such visions are not backed up by present scientific knowledge, as I will try to show. Moreover, no one would care to prophesy anything really more definite than the fact that the next ten years of flying will far outstrip the last.

The Aeroplane in War.

Probably, in these times of a world's rush to rearm, the aeroplane takes first place in our minds as an instrument to kill. The finest brains, best material, and millions of money are being used to manufacture thousands of fast fighters, long-range bombers, quick-firing guns, high explosive torpedoes and bombs. Tens of thousands of men are being trained to outdo each other in dealing out death. Spain and China have served as the experimental aerial battlefields for future wars. We have grown used to reading of air-raids on helpless cities, of the slaughter of old men, women, and children, of fire and destruction, disease and pestilence.

Our warplanes are doing speeds of 362 m.p.h.[1] and climbing to heights of 11,000 feet in five minutes, whilst our commercial planes are still hobbling along at a hundred miles an hour. The flower of our country's youth is being pressed into military service, whilst our commercial airlines and flying-schools are crying out for pilots and instruc-

[1] The latest supermarine Spitfires.

tors. New Royal Air Force flying-fields are being constructed daily, whilst our airports are being closed down one by one.

Where is it all going to end ? In another war to end wars ? Or in a war which will end us ? Discussion and controversy rage backwards and forwards, like a shuttlecock across a net, on the relative virtues of the fighter versus the bomber ; the utility or stupidity of the balloon barrage ; the best methods of precaution against air-raids ; the relative dangers of poison gases, incendiary bombs, and high explosive shells, and so on.

It is outside the scope of this book to go into the pros and cons of such arguments, nor have I the space or inclination to write of the horrors of poison gas, real and imagined, of death-rays, of fumes sprayed from the air to deprive the civilian population of movement and memory, of new death-dealing engines and metals, and such-like ghastly visions of the modern writer of fiction and plays.

Serious thinking men write reasoned truths.

Professor J. B. S. Haldane, in a lecture he gave recently to the Royal United Services Institution, expressed the firm opinion that much nonsense is talked and written about the terrible things that are going to happen in future wars. He thinks it very unlikely that anything worse than mustard gas will be produced (some people, of course, wonder if there *can* be anything worse than mustard gas), or that explosives will get much worse, as there is a limit to the amount of energy which can be put into a given weight, or that disease will be spread by spraying microbes from aeroplanes. This is so difficult, he says, that high explosive shells will probably be found easier and more effective.

I have even read recently a case for the *defence* of bombing! The point of view taken is that, 'If thirty thousand men, fine and young, straight and strong, die to-morrow in some battle it will rate but a paragraph in our news. But if a city is bombed and one thousand of the city's inhabitants are killed—the aged, the weak, the nerveless child—the headlines will scream.

'The war of the future is no longer confined to the battle zone, no longer can it be isolated to within a few miles of a given line. And with this fact slowly being discovered by all, I can see the ultimate arrival of a real and lasting peace. . . . The bombing aeroplane heralds a new peace.' [1]

In any event, one fact, taught us by the wars of Abyssinia, Spain, and China, is indisputable, and that is, that the air arm, though it will undoubtedly

[1] T. Wewege-Smith, in *The Aeroplane*, 28th December 1938.

play the most important part in any future conflict, cannot of itself decide the issue. Territory, to be won, must be occupied, and aeroplanes cannot occupy a territory. They might drop troops by parachute, but hardly in sufficient numbers to play a decisive part.

Let us hope that all this frantic planning and preparation, this pouring out of talent and money, may yet be turned to account for our country's welfare.

In any event, for the purpose of looking into the future, I will take this point of view, for it is decidedly more pleasant to play the optimist.

Flying High.

First of all, let us take a glimpse upward into the stratosphere and guess how high we shall fly tomorrow.

Our present planes usually fly between heights of 2000 and 10,000 feet, because we have not yet in actual service the type of plane which can take advantage of those conditions which prevail at greater heights. Such machines can be built, and are in process of experimental construction, but nowhere yet is the high altitude transport aeroplane in actual use on an airline. It is, however, not very difficult to forecast that, within the next ten years, all the world's major air routes will be operated by such high-speed planes flying at great heights in regions of perpetually fine weather.

At the present time, the height at which a plane flies is usually dependent on the wind and the weather, and sometimes, too, on the regulations of the particular country over which it is flying. For example, in England, the minimum legal height for an aeroplane over towns is 2000 feet, whilst over the Channel it is recommended, though not enforced, that a single-engined plane should fly at a height of at least 6000 feet, so that in the event of engine failure he will have sufficient height to glide to the coast.

In America commercial planes have to fly at certain fixed altitudes. Flying westwards, they must be over 6000 feet altitude and keep on levels of even numbers of thousand feet. On the eastward trip, the minimum height required is 5000 feet, and planes must keep to the levels of odd numbers of thousand feet. This makes collisions on the busy trans-continental airways impossible. Usually American planes fly at greater heights than do ours, as designs are further advanced, and for many years variable pitch propellers, supercharged engines, and high octane fuel—all essential for altitude flying—have been in regular use. In fact, research work was started along these lines as long ago as 1920.

First, however, a word about the stratosphere, and in particular the substratosphere, where air routes of the future will mainly be found.

It is amazing how few people know that it is the balloon, and not the aeroplane, which has played the most important part in the conquest of the stratosphere. This can readily be understood once it is realised that the aeroplane depends on air for its propulsion, engine, and cooling, and to give it 'lift' to fly at all. As everyone knows, the higher you go the less air there is, and therefore an aeroplane's 'ceiling' necessarily depends on the amount of air it needs and the amount it can get.

The limiting factor of the ceiling of a balloon is totally different. It depends principally on the size of the balloon. The weight is of importance, too, because, although the lifting power of the bag always stays in front of its weight (on the theory that balloon volume increases by the cube of the diameter, whilst the weight increases only by the square), yet it is useless for a balloon to be sent up without scientific instruments, ballast (without which the balloon cannot descend safely), a crew, and a gondola. It is not strictly necessary for men to go up in the balloon, but there will always be scientists, like Professor Piccard, who must explore in person, and in any event they can put their experiences into words to humanise the figures and data of instruments. In addition to this, a 'manned' balloon can stay aloft longer, and from the scientific point of view this is important for the study of cosmic rays.

Small unmanned balloons are sent up, equipped with 'robot' observers, scientific instruments, and mechanical and photographic recording apparatus. The balloon stays up for three to four hours, and, when it reaches a certain height, it bursts and the instruments glide down to the ground attached to parachutes.

On 19th November 1938 six such balloons were sent up from the Franklin Institute, Philadelphia, U.S.A. It was ingeniously contrived that the instruments carried should communicate their readings to two radio ground stations by means of electrical impulses to a tiny radio transmitter. One of the balloons was actually recovered on 21st November in the Atlantic Ocean, eight miles off the coast of Massachusetts, with a note in a waterproof case asking for it to be returned to the Institute.

A balloon goes up only because it weighs less than the air it displaces. Therefore, not only is its size controlled by the weight it has to carry, as explained above, but a limit to this size is quickly reached as it climbs into the upper reaches of thin air, where gigantic dimensions would be needed.

Till now, rubberised cotton has been used for the fabric of the stratosphere balloon on account of its strength. If some lighter, but equally strong, material could be found, the weight of the bag would be reduced considerably and the altitude record would conceivably creep up a little. Expert opinion, however, is that the present record of approximately 14 miles will not be exceeded by more than a mile at most. It is calculated that to double the present record 2500 tons weight would have to be lifted.

Professor Piccard, however, is more optimistic and has a still unsatisfied ambition to reach a height of 30,000 metres (18·641 miles).

The name of Professor Auguste Piccard, a Swiss Professor at the University of Brussels, is famous the world over for his daring ascents into the stratosphere. It was his first ascent, in August 1931, with his assistant Paul Kipfer, which really started a new era for the balloon—that of stratosphere research. He rose to a height of 9·81 miles—the first man to enter the stratosphere.

Previous attempts had failed principally because the crews had perished from lack of oxygen. Professor Piccard solved the problem with a sealed gondola, in which the air pressure was kept at normal level, just as it is in a submarine, except that for deep-sea work the walls of the submarine must be made to withstand terrific pressure from without, whilst the stratosphere machine, or gondola, has to be strong enough to keep from bursting from the greater pressure *inside*.

The primary purpose of the balloonist is scientific, but the aeroplane seeks the higher levels for military and economic purposes. The balloonist, therefore, besides obtaining information on all kinds of rays which vitally influence not only mankind, but our climate and vegetable life, is helping aeroplane and engine designers by providing them with valuable observations on air pressures, densities, temperatures, and the like, as well as a knowledge of meteorological conditions in the upper regions which are important to the stratosphere navigator.

The Rocket.

As I have tried to explain, there is a limit to both aeroplane and balloon exploration, and, when that is reached, the rocket will come into its own and carry on an apparently limitless investigation. Whether we shall ever have week-end flights to the planets it is impossible to forecast, but the limiting factor would appear to be not so much the difficulty of getting there as the impossibility of living there once you had arrived. It would seem fairly certain, however, that rocket flights from place to place on our own globe are within the realms of possibility. Every day I seem to be picking up books in which something or other which has been deemed ‘ unlikely ’ or ‘ impossible ’ has nevertheless come to pass. Very often certain forecasts of ancient times, rejected and ridiculed at the time, are the very ones to be translated into truth to-day. It would seem stupid, therefore, either to repudiate or to scoff at some of the seemingly fantastic visions of to-day.

For example, H. G. Wells in *The First Men in the Moon* causes gravity to be overcome so that a rocket flight can be made to the moon. An engineer discovers a substance which renders weightless all objects which come under its shadow. That is all very well for a novel, but scientists say that it is impossible to remove gravity, and that to break through the earth's gravitational field an initial velocity of 12,250 yards per second is needed, an acceleration which no human being could endure. And yet—experiments are being made even to-day to overcome gravity, that strange force which we do not understand but whose power we decidedly feel and which so successfully limits our gropings into the infinite. From wishes and dreams often materialises an idea which, as science progresses, finally becomes a crystallised fact, as in very truth happened in the conquest of the air itself.

Rockets figure largely in myths and legends of the past. Sir Isaac Newton then came to wave the wand of science over this vision of conquering interstellar space. To-day his successors translate his scientific theory into the action of the rocket. Experiments are actually being carried out and rocket flights have been made in many countries, notably by Professor Goddard in America, but the 'Great Flight to the Moon' still remains unaccomplished.

Professor Piccard believes that the splitting of the atom and the harnessing of its powers to science will be the means of supplying the key to the problem of interplanetary flight.

With a rocket-ship a modern Jules Verne could circle the globe in twenty-four hours, cross the Atlantic in three, breakfast in England and dine in Australia.

The 'Stratosphere' Plane.

Before giving a few details of the experimental passenger-carrying 'stratosphere' planes being built to-day, just let me say a few words about the stratosphere itself, so that you can appreciate some of the problems involved.

The air is warmest near the earth, due to contact with its surface, the air transmitting heat at a greater rate than it absorbs it, and therefore the further away the air is from the earth's surface the cooler it becomes. The temperature falls on an average at the rate of 3 degrees per 1000 feet of altitude.

This goes on under ordinary conditions until the 'tropopause' is reached, which is the name given to the boundary layer of variable air extending for two or three miles separating the lower atmosphere (or 'troposphere,' as the scientists term it) from the stratosphere.

The troposphere extends upwards to an approximate height of seven miles, but this varies according to the latitude, the season, and pressure. At the poles it is higher (approximately ten miles) than at the Equator (approximately six miles). It is also higher in summer than in winter.

The stratosphere, mostly composed of hydrogen, extends upwards to a height of anything from thirty to fifty miles, whilst still higher up are other layers which do not concern us here.

In Great Britain the 'floor' of the stratosphere is at approximately eight miles. The height record for an aeroplane to-day (56,000 feet) is only just inside the stratosphere. It is considered that this cannot be very much improved upon with our present internal combustion engine.

The trend of the commercial aeroplane of the future will be to climb as high as possible into the stratosphere, which is a calm region free from clouds and weather changes, with no seasons, a constant temperature the whole year round and where the rarefied air offers little resistance. However, the very fact that the air becomes thinner and thinner, offering ever less resistance to the attainment of incredible speeds, is at the same time the factor limiting the petrol air-cooled engine for which air is vitally necessary.

America is probably further ahead than any other country with designs for a commercial 'Stratosphere' plane. Most of the engineering problems have been solved, and the greatest problem is that of 'supercharging' the cabin for the comfort of passengers. Designers are aiming at a height of 30,000 feet, which is some two miles below the 'floor' of the stratosphere and falls within the 'tropopause.' Here temperature is constant, wind speeds low, and practically no climatic changes are experienced, even though some of the highest cirrus sometimes extend as high as 40,000 feet. In this attenuated air speeds will be higher and fuel consumption lower, whilst 'pay-load' will almost double itself.

America's designs include the Boeing 'Stratoliner,' a 33-passenger plane (with sleeping berths to accommodate 25 for night-flights). Four supercharged Wright Cyclone engines, with Hamilton three-bladed variable pitch propellers, will operate this sleekly streamlined shining metal monoplane at a height of 20,000 feet. This is a 'compromise' height with the stratosphere proper.

Pressure-regulating apparatus in the cabin will give the passengers normal air to breathe and the precautions taken to make everything absolutely airtight will, at the same time, help to make the cabin almost sound-proof.

Well do I remember a test flight I had some two or three years ago in America in the latest Douglas plane of the time, in which sound-proofing of the cabin had been made a speciality. So quiet was it that the passengers were able to converse together in ordinary tones. The press report was amusing: 'At 10,000 feet, speeding along at a hundred and seventy miles an hour, the cabin was so amazingly quiet that, sitting in front, I could distinctly hear the low conversation of the people at the back.'

The Boeing Company is also building a 73-

passenger flying-boat to carry a crew of eight, freight up to 4555 lbs., with a range of 1500 miles. If the pay-load is converted into fuel, the boats will easily be able to cross the North Atlantic with a full load of passengers. No doubt those are the plans of Pan-American Airways, for which company the boats have been ordered.

In this country we have just reached the stage where commercial planes are beginning to do over 200 m.p.h. Our military planes are climbing to ever greater heights and increasing their speeds daily, but so far as civil flying is concerned, progress has recently been almost at a standstill. We are not even installing sleeping berths in our latest air-liners (although most aircraft designers are allowing for them in their interior layout) because our air routes are not yet equipped for all-night flying; whilst, as for stratosphere, or even sub-stratosphere, machines, there is at the moment only one type definitely ordered for regular use on an airline, and that is the new Fairey F.C. 1 airliners now under construction to the order of British Airways. Not only is it a revolutionary step of some significance that such a famous manufacturing firm of military aircraft should enter the civil aviation field, but the machine itself is of very advanced design. The cabin is to be sealed and pressure-proof and air-conditioned for high altitude flying, whilst the speed is estimated to be in the region of 275 m.p.h.

In England, development of landplanes has largely been in the hands of the De Havilland Aircraft Company Ltd., who now have on the market two types of airliners of excellent design and performance, which should do much to regain for us the commercial markets we have fast been losing to America. These two types are the twin-engined Flamingo, a medium capacity high-speed liner, about half the size of the four-engined 13-ton Albatross type. Two Bristol Perseus XIIc 850 h.p. engines give the Flamingo a cruising speed of over 200 m.p.h. On short journeys twenty passengers can be carried, but for longer stages the seating is rearranged to instal adjustable armchairs and give plenty of room for from twelve to seventeen passengers. The Air Ministry has recently ordered several machines of this type for communications work in the Royal Air Force.

The Albatross type has four Gipsy 12 twelve-cylinder engines, with De Havilland controllable-pitch constant-speed airscrews. It is designed to cruise at 11,000 feet, where it attains its most economical cruising speed of 210 m.p.h. with full load. As the service ceiling is only 17,900 feet, this machine does not aim at anything like stratosphere flight, nor is the cabin pressure-proof. Beautifully streamlined, it is a type, however, which could probably easily be adapted to really high altitude flying, and that is undoubtedly the next step forward the De Havilland Company will make.

The machine is equipped with anti-icing equipment, automatic pilot, all-wave two-way radio and blind-approach receiver, accommodation for 22 passengers, and a kitchen, whilst a conversion into a sleeper coach for overnight travel can easily be made during a refuelling halt, as it only takes a few minutes to give each passenger a separate sleeper compartment.

Imperial Airways have now in service several machines of this type, which they call the 'Frobisher' class. The Armstrong-Whitworth 'Ensign' is already doing good work in the hands of Imperial Airways, and the twin-engined Percival Q6 is a very popular type for charter and taxi work, 'feeder' services, and as a private owner's machine (for those who can afford it).

Britain is second to none so far as her flying-boats are concerned, and the famous company of Short Bros. is building huge flying-boats for Imperial Airways service across the North Atlantic. These boats are being designed to refuel in the air. As a matter of interest, so keen is the competition to be amongst the passengers on the first commercial crossing, that Imperial Airways have already a hundred people down on the waiting-list. Such is the faith we have to-day in aviation!

So far as the passengers themselves are concerned, high altitude flying will be far more comfortable for them, as they will be above most of the 'bumps' which make flying in the lower atmosphere sometimes so unpleasant. As against this, the monotony and boredom of a long trans-ocean flight will be great, and it is certain that some forms of amusement will have to be contrived to while away the tedious hours.

Although, theoretically, there is no limit to the size of an aircraft, yet it is the general opinion amongst aircraft designers and airline operators that a larger number of smaller planes making a high frequency of service possible is more economical and practical than a few huge unwieldy machines costing a fortune to build and maintain. (It should be noticed that flying-boats need not be limited in size by consideration of aerodrome problems, as landplanes necessarily are, which is one of the reasons why flying-boats of all countries are, in general, larger than their landplanes).

Because of this limiting factor of aerodromes it is likely that landplanes will not exceed some 50 to

100 tons for the next twenty-five years, whilst flying-boats are already being planned to carry 100 tons and more.

Such a boat could cross the Atlantic in less than twenty hours, and would have comfortable staterooms, a dining saloon where games and dancing would take place in the evenings, promenade decks, smoking lounges, a library, and, in general, such luxuries as you would normally expect to find on a yacht or first-class liner.

To sum up, therefore, it would seem that the tendency of the immediate future is to increase the size, speed, 'ceiling,' and range of commercial aircraft, all such factors, however, being more limited in landplane than in flying-boat construction. The landplane design must still be a matter of compromise between airport and aircraft designers, whilst flying-boats will only be limited by questions of economy and practicability. However, it is always dangerous to forecast in these days of rapid change, and the discovery of some new substance or metal or the use of some new fuel, such as liquid hydrogen, would revolutionise the whole picture.

Future Air Routes.

It is easy enough to work out in theory how quickly we can get from place to place, given the speed of the plane and the distance between the two places. It is also easy to draw on the map a straight line between these two places and call this the air route.

In practice, however, the *average* speed works out considerably lower, and the straight line often has to be given a decided kink.

From the actual cruising speed of the plane must be deducted time for 'delays,' such as spending the night in hotels instead of in a sleeping berth while being speeded on your way (this is where we lose the most time on our own trunk airlines, though we could avoid it if the routes were equipped for night-flying); refuelling (essential delay, but could be speeded up considerably); making detours to pick up passengers or to land on a suitable aerodrome for refuelling (these 'delays' could be avoided by 'feeder' lines and more and better aerodromes); time wasted in climbing to cross some mountain range or to clear a patch of bad weather (could be avoided if high altitude machines were used, when not only would their operation be the most economical but at the same time all obstacles of earth and weather would be safely cleared).

K.L.M. are now planning a twice-weekly service between Croydon and Australia, to commence early in 1940, with a service of 3½ days in each direction.

The present time is 8 days. The latest Douglas landplanes will be used, with accommodation for 42 passengers by day and 24 by night in sleeping berths. All-day and all-night flying will, of course, be the rule.

Our plans do not yet include all-night flying, although we are speeding up the day schedule with Short flying-boats, which have the great advantage of being able to keep to British waters and therefore avoid detours enforced by the regulations of certain foreign countries.

So far as the immediate future is concerned, in all countries the main problems are connected with weather, especially fog and icing-up. Blind-flying instruments, and training to use them, are adequate for our present-day machines, but there is still room for improvement in directional radio and for more foolproof methods of bringing a plane down to earth in fog. Various methods are used, chief amongst them being the Lorenz system, while all are dependent on radio help. I have practised a Lorenz 'blind' landing on the Link trainer (a small model machine used for training purposes, which duplicates exactly all the instruments on a large multi-engined airliner, and the conditions of air through which it flies), and my only difficulty was hearing the signals. It is essential that some means be found of reserving certain bands of wireless waves solely for aircraft. Not only are planes dependent on wireless signals for being brought safely to land in fog, but meteorological reports, distress signals, directional signals and important messages all require a service undisturbed by static and other interruptions.

There is, too, a new altimeter undergoing test, which, by means of wireless waves, will tell the pilot his height above *any* land, not just his height above sea-level. Such an altimeter, if reliable, would make fog-flying and landing infinitely safer.

The dangers of ice-formation are very great, and in spite of experiments in every country, no satisfactory solution has yet been found. Obviously, when ice forms on the leading edges of the plane's wings and propellers, not only is the weight increased, but the streamlined efficiency of the aeroplane is lowered. Ice forms in certain conditions of temperature and humidity, and even though the pilot tries to get through the danger zone as rapidly as possible, the ice piles up at a most alarming rate.

So far as forced landings or landings in fog are concerned, a modern contrivance of a forward wheel under the nose of the machine is proving extremely helpful. The machine is thus literally able to ' fly into the ground ' at the ordinary gliding angle with the engine just ticking over. Popularly the device is known as the 'tricycle undercarriage,' and it was originally only used in small light planes as it was not thought possible to make the front wheel strong enough to support the nose of some huge airliner. However, recent experiments with the twin-engined Douglas planes have been very successful.

Taking it for granted that all these 'delays' will, in course of time, be eradicated, or at least diminished, let us turn to the air routes themselves.

There is no doubt that commercial aviation must be international and that much 'give and take' is required from each and every country. Reciprocal agreements are being signed almost daily, always with one eye on future economic progress and the other on military considerations.

Pan-American Airways and Imperial Airways are co-operating in the North Atlantic; British Airways have signed agreements with the Governments of Portugal and South America for operational powers in the South Atlantic; for years Imperial Airways have co-operated with airlines in Australia over the England–Australia route, and so on.

The tendency will inevitably be towards co-operation rather than competition, for there will be traffic enough for all. The fastest lines will probably take first-class traffic at somewhat higher cost, and the slower ones may operate a 'tourist' traffic at attractive rates.

A further tendency will probably be for large machines to be used on through main routes, with many feeder lines running from the main junctions. The 'feeder' planes will be smaller, slower, operating with great frequency of service, but landing often (taking the place of the 'slow' train). There are already in existence several main trunk lines, as I have outlined in other chapters, but we do not yet have enough branch lines, nor frequent nor fast enough services on any line, main or branch.

The future will probably bring daily services to Australia, to South Africa, to the Far East, to New York, and to South America. Daily 'express' services of, say, three days to Australia and two days to Cape Town should be possible. Slower schedules could also be run, forming a kind of cheaper 'second-class' service.

Even to-day there is practically no spot on the earth which cannot be reached by aeroplane, and most places can be reached by use of the ordinary commercial lines.

However, there is still room for more lines and more frequent services. Besides the actual efficiency of the plane itself, there is, too, the all-important question of ground equipment, and this plays a large share in progress.

For example, larger aerodromes would help, unmarred by high obstacles around. The ideal aerodrome is a level piece of ground of 700 acres, with 4000-feet runways allowing landings from six different directions, and space for roads, car-parks, hotel and airport buildings. The cost of such an aerodrome, if situated near to a metropolitan area, would be almost prohibitive, which is often the reason why the airport is either too small or too far away. The next step will undoubtedly have to come from the aircraft designers in reducing landing speeds and increasing gliding angles, so that obstacles near the landing area can be given a wider berth.

It would further seem not only desirable but essential to light up all high obstacles such as wireless masts, tall chimneys, unusually high gasometers, and so on. Far too many accidents have resulted from crashing into high obstacles in fog or at night, but not even yet are all such objects illuminated, as they ought to be.

It would be a great help if weather reports were given out regularly by wireless, as is the system in America, and a further aid to pilots would undoubtedly be an 'air chart' showing dangerous air-currents, much as ocean currents are indicated on a marine chart. At first sight this may not seem very important, but many accidents have happened because of an unexpected and violent down-draught resulting from some particular air conditions not understood or realised by the pilot. For example, it is fairly well established that the airship R 101, which crashed to its fate on the hills near Beauvais, lost its height in the down-draught from the hills. In any event, whether this was the actual cause of the crash or not, the explanation is a plausible one.

All glider pilots are familiar with such air-currents, and are unlikely to be trapped in the violent eddies found amongst mountain ranges, or even sometimes when coming in to land at their home airport! This book is not concerned with the art and usefulness of gliding, but suffice it to say that many of the major nations are including a course of gliding in the airline pilot's curriculum.

So much, then, for the immediate future of the world's airlines. The more distant future may well bring rocket services to North and South Poles, around the world, so that Europe could be reached from America overnight, Australia the next day, Asia the next, and three to four-day tours round the world might constitute the business man's holiday. But why ? is the question I ask myself. Personally, I would rather laze on some secluded beach for a holiday than indulge in a crowded rush round the world or freeze at either of the Poles. It is, anyway, all a question of taste and the world fortunately is made up of all sorts.

There remains only to say a word about the future of private flying, that much-abused little sister of commercial and military aviation.

Will the poor man ever have his aeroplane ? Will aeroplanes become as common as motor-cars ? Both are popular questions, judging by the number of times I am bombarded with them.

My answer is 'No' to both.

Aeroplanes can never become as useful as motor-cars, if only because of the problems of take-off and landing. Even if the autogyro is perfected, so that speed, range and carrying power can be combined with vertical landings and take-off, still a piece of ground as large as a cricket pitch would be needed. Perhaps the future of town planning may be made to accommodate a cricket pitch per citizen, but I doubt it.

Further, the traffic problems would be enormous, and, until planes can be made to hover so that they could wait in a queue for the 'green aerial traffic light,' I do not see any way of marshalling hundreds of thousands of aeroplanes at one time. The problems have been only partially and not very successfully solved even so far as road transport is concerned, never mind extending the troubles to the air.

The answer to the second question also settles the first, because, unless aeroplanes are really made in vast quantities, the cost can never appreciably come down, and therefore the poor man cannot afford them. Privately owned aeroplanes will remain a luxury, in my opinion, and will more nearly approximate to the idea of the motor-boat than to the motor-car.

The actual cost of learning to fly has recently been considerably reduced by the inauguration of the Government's Civil Air Guard scheme, but even this is a scheme designed rather to provide a large reserve of pilots for military purposes than merely to foster private flying, nor does it in any way help the newly-fledged pilot to own his machine or even to hire one apart from his ordinary school training.

Therefore, the cost of learning to fly still remains prohibitively high for the majority wishful of flying for business or merely for pleasure, and the cost of buying and of maintaining a private aeroplane is impossible for all but a very wealthy few. I have owned planes myself and I know what I am talking about. Not only is there the initial cost of the plane, but in addition there are maintenance charges (compulsory, especially the yearly overhaul for the Certificate of Airworthiness), cost of high-grade petrol (much of which is tax, ostensibly for the Road Fund! in France, this is returned to the pilot) and oil, insurance (extremely high), hangarage fees (far higher than garage charges), landing fees, and all the other expenses coincident with travelling.

Added to all this expense there are such problems as finding your way around. Private users of wireless are not welcomed and in any event have to take second place if an airliner needs attention, and, whilst aerial maps are in every way excellent, yet finding your way in poor visibility is very hazardous, as witness the number of forced landings and crashes due to people getting lost and coming down low to read the name on some railway station or making an actual landing in some field to make inquiries. Aerodromes are too scarce and the time taken to get to your ultimate destination even after you have safely landed is too long. These and other troubles could quite easily be solved with a little official help and co-operation. For example, it would be very easy to sign-post the country by painting the names of towns on railway sleepers (easily blacked out in time of emergency).

Personally, I do not now own an aeroplane because it is too expensive. I glide, however, because it is peaceful, cheap and much more interesting than 'power' flying.

Apart from the contentious question of private flying, there is no doubt whatever that aviation is a major force in our national, economic and military life, and that if we do not recognise this we are not in step with the times. My most fervent wish is that the aeroplane will very soon have its chance to develop as an instrument to foster international trade and to enrich a lasting Peace.

CPSIA information can be obtained at www.ICGtesting.com
Printed in the USA
LVOW130756091112

306562LV00001B/12/P